The Executive MBA
for Engineers
and Scientists

OTHER AUERBACH PUBLICATIONS

The Executive MBA for Engineers and Scientists

James J. Farley

CRC Press
Taylor & Francis Group
Boca Raton   London   New York

CRC Press is an imprint of the
Taylor & Francis Group, an **informa** business
AN AUERBACH BOOK

CRC Press
Taylor & Francis Group
6000 Broken Sound Parkway NW, Suite 300
Boca Raton, FL 33487-2742

First issued in paperback 2017

© 2010 by Taylor and Francis Group, LLC
CRC Press is an imprint of Taylor & Francis Group, an Informa business

No claim to original U.S. Government works

ISBN 13: 978-1-138-11430-2 (pbk)
ISBN 13: 978-1-4398-0099-7 (hbk)

Library of Congress Cataloging-in-Publication Data

Farley, James J.
    The executive MBA for engineers and scientists / James J. Farley. -- 2nd. ed.
       p. cm.
    Includes index.
    ISBN 978-1-4398-0099-7 (hardcover : alk. paper)
    1. Management. 2. Profit. I. Title.

HD31.F24 2010
658--dc22
                                           2009035199

Visit the Taylor & Francis Web site at
http://www.taylorandfrancis.com

and the CRC Press Web site at
http://www.crcpress.com

To Marilyn, an extraordinary person, my wife.

Contents

Preface

This book is written primarily for the aspiring technical manager on the way up the ladder. This technical manager may be brilliant in chemistry, physics, biology, or engineering; however, this person will—as he or she climbs the ladder—find that business skills are needed. He or she does not need buzz words; they will not suffice. At this point in a career, for the good of the person and for the good of the company, business savvy (not business jargon) is what is needed.

Business today represents the merging of technological developments with market demand and, hence, a knowledge of technology and the business principles (and their actual applications) is needed in order to maximize profits. The phrase "maximize profits" will be mentioned frequently in this book because that's what business is all about—to make a profit and to make the highest possible profit within the realms of time, economics, and ethics.

In the preparation of this text, I have tried to adhere strictly to the title and describe those business principles and applications that are most important for the technical manager to understand. This book is not meant to be a compilation of textbooks on each of the individual subjects of marketing, economics, etc. If the reader wants to buy a textbook about any of the individual chapter headings or topics, a sufficient number of good ones are available. Rather, this book is intended to be what I believe may be *the first book of its kind* that touches on "just enough" of each of the topics to give the reader an adequate understanding.

Parts I and II describe business and the technical functions along with their individual elements or topics. Part III shows the integration of these elements to achieve the goal of selling a company's product or service, hopefully at a price greater than the cost to produce, to generate a profit for the company. Once in a while a company sells a product at a price below the cost to produce. This results in a loss. On rare occasions such sales are deliberate, to allow another product line to profit directly or indirectly. Sometimes, however, the loss is not realized until after the fact and rapid adjustments must be made. Part IV is called Planning Ahead and the chapters discuss planning and moving ahead in your career as a company person or as the owner of your own business.

This book is meant to be a *practical* guide and is based on my true-to-life experiences and observations. Since my career is in the pharmaceutical industry, including work with the Food and Drug Administration, many of the examples in the text are from pharmaceutical situations. However, similar situations occur in all the other industries. Problems in other industries are identified and solved with the same techniques.

Throughout this book, a product or service will be referred to as a product to avoid overuse of verbiage. If your company provides a service, the same considerations apply. In most situations the "he" or "his" pronoun is used. Continually referring to "he or she" or "he/she" would be distracting, so the male pronoun is used most of the time. We all know that women are as capable as men and have no need to prove it here by complicating the text. You, reader, may see various places where a particular topic could have been treated in a different chapter. Several topics apply to more than one chapter. They overlap various subjects and the selection of the chapters in which they were placed was on a *best fit* basis.

A review of the content of this book will show that it is more than a book for the technical manager who wants to master business subjects. It is also intended to serve as a very good reference for business persons on the move upward in sales, marketing, manufacturing, and other areas, who must learn about technological functions. In fact, I believe that if both business managers and technical staff read this book, they can attend meetings that will be much shorter, achieve greater communication, and feel a sense of accomplishment upon leaving those meetings.

The reader can use this book as a reference in communicating and negotiating with people in other areas within and outside of the company. This text will enable the reader to know more about the overall integrated functions of a company, be more productive to the company, and progress up the ladder to find personal achievement and reward.

People skills and communication are emphasized throughout this book. Despite all the newest technology available today, communications innovations like e-mail, smart phones, and the like are tools; we should use such tools properly, not let the tools use us. Ultimately, we deal with people who use both our products and other people's products. While many business factors have changed in recent years, people have not. They remain the same. They are the most variable on an individual basis, yet collectively remain the same. They can be frustrating to deal with, and they can be immensely gratifying to deal with. They can be steady or capricious. The more you know about them and yourself, the more fascinating and rewarding life and your career can be.

This is written as an *easy-to-read* book discussing principles that are of *immediate and practical application*. Sit back and enjoy. Hopefully you will have the feeling that I am sitting at a table with you and, maybe over coffee, talking directly to you. Practice the skills and techniques presented here and watch good things happen.

JAMES J. FARLEY

Acknowledgments

There are several persons whose assistance should be recognized. They helped me directly, over the phone, or through correspondence and by sending me encouraging notes during the writing of this book.

Alan R. Tripp, author of *Millions from the Mind*, enlightened me about some ideas. He was most helpful, even beyond this book, with ideas and encouragement for various projects involving product development and advertising.

Dr. Sametria McFall, director of continuing education at Savannah State University, has an understanding of what working persons need in the areas of education and training. I appreciate her insights and comments.

Paul Hawken, former principal of Smith and Hawken Company, Mill Valley, California, and author of *Growing a Business*, permitted me to include his thoughts.

Thanks to Steve Koniers for many of the illustrations.

I mention last, but certainly not least, special thanks to Marilyn S. Farley for constructive suggestions, several good ideas, and proofreading. For an author, a spouse who has a degree in journalism from The Pennsylvania State University is a genuine asset.

Thank you all for your encouragement and information.

Author

Jim Farley has worked in the pharmaceutical and pharmaceutical packaging industries for more than 40 years. His industry, academic, federal government, and consulting experiences combine to provide a unique background and view that Jim utilizes in his everyday business and technical activities. He has managed a quality control laboratory and a technical service department, and formed and directed a research and development laboratory in industry.

Jim was employed as Director of the Science Branch of the Philadelphia District of the U.S. Food and Drug Administration before starting his own business, Cardinal Consulting and Training, which assists pharmaceutical and biotechnology firms in the technical, regulatory, and business aspects of bringing their new drugs to the market.

Jim has an MS in physical chemistry and an MBA in marketing and finance and uses that dual background to teach the symbiosis of the technical and business areas in training seminars for clients and for several professional training organizations.

Jim was an adjunct instructor at two of The Pennsylvania State University's Philadelphia area campuses, where he instructed various management subjects. He also taught physical chemistry at Rosemont College, finance and marketing at Cabrini College, and physical chemistry at St. Joseph's University in Philadelphia. He was an instructor in the graduate school of Temple University in Philadelphia, teaching specific courses related to FDA regulatory affairs.

Jim currently resides in Savannah, Georgia, where he directs the activities of Cardinal Consulting and Training.

PART I
THE ELEMENTS

1

BUSINESS

An Overview

A business is formed and exists so that its owners can produce and sell a product or service to yield proceeds of more value than the costs to produce and sell it. This leads to what is called a profit.

Some firms don't do this. They sell at a figure below their costs to produce and deliver the items. Some firms sell below cost deliberately and call the product a "loss leader"—it is sold at a loss on the premise that purchasing customers will see other items sold by the same firm and buy them with a resulting net profit to the firm. Some, however, sell at a loss and don't realize it until it's too late. Obviously not good!

Before this happens to you, let's look at the fundamental principle of business, the reason it exists, the *raison d'être* (pronounced rā zōn dĕt´rə). You should understand the very basic tenets of business before going any further. After we master the core idea, we will then go on to the interrelationships of the various business areas.

Fundamental principle of business: A person who wants money offers to provide a service or product for a person who has the money. They agree, and upon completion of the transfer of the service or product, the person who has the money gives it to the person who wants the money. This way both parties are satisfied.

Keep in mind that "the person having the money calls the shots" before giving the money to the person who wants the money. It's that simple!

Let's look at the steps of the transaction. Person P provides a product or service (he is also called the provider). Person C wants the product or service and has the money (he is also called a client or customer). Person P agrees to provide the product or service to Person C in exchange for the money. Person C agrees to the terms of the proposed arrangement. Person P provides the product or service to Person C and receives the money for it.

That's it! The process is that simple! Other factors may need to be considered, but in essence doing business requires following these simple steps. That's what business is all about: providing something someone needs or wants in exchange for money.

What other factors should be considered? Let's list them.

First, the product or service should be exactly as agreed regarding quality and delivery.

Second, the time of payment must be determined. In a restaurant, food is paid for after it is consumed. A movie is paid for before it is viewed in a movie theatre. In contracting work such as constructing a building, an "up-front" payment is usually made, and then subsequent payments are made throughout the performance of the contract.

Third, the provider and customer must agree who will determine whether the quality of the product is correct; the determination may be made by the customer or his agent such as a quality control manager employed by the customer's company.

Fourth, quality level, price, and delivery terms must be understood before the contract is entered into. This function falls into the area of project management.

The fifth point includes the other four: conduct business with the highest degree of ethics. If you do, all other aspects of business will fall into place and you will find that your customers will refer you more customers.

Deliver What You Promise. On Time!

Let's jump ahead. You now have a thriving business with several employees. You no longer do business as an individual. Those employees have assigned responsibilities. You have payroll, insurance for them, and several other matters to consider. You are selling more and making more money. However, the Person P to Person C interchange still exists. It is simply achieved through your designated employees instead of directly with you. The premise of delivering what you promise—on time—still applies.

Let's jump further ahead. As time passes, your business expands and you now have your own building, in fact two of them, in different cities. You have all the work and all the rewards that you did previously (of course you do; why would you have expanded if you were not being rewarded?) and now you also face more local regulations. The Person P to Person C interchange still exists, through your designated employees at the multiple locations instead of directly with you. "Deliver what you promise. On time!" still applies.

More time elapses and your business has grown so large that you decide to subcontract some of the work to outside contractors. This means more contracts, more people involved, more money made. The Person P to Person C interchange still exists. So does "Deliver what you promise. On time!"

This series of scenarios can continue until you become the chief executive officer (CEO) of a multi-billion dollar corporation. The size of the company and the amount of money change; the obligations do not. As CEO, you are still Person P. You cannot say that the company is Person P. You are. The company is not a person. It exists as an entity on paper and you represent it. Never forget that. And "Deliver what you promise. On time!"

Indeed, you can and should expect the same performances of others with whom you have dealings when you are their customer. In fact, it is best to not deal with persons who do not meet your standards. They don't deserve your business and you deserve better providers. By now you see that certain aspects of business do not change. These apply to all businesses all the time. Your product or service is to be used by a customer (Person C). The Person P (you) to Person C (customer) interchange still exists. The company's expansions have not changed that. "Deliver What You Promise, On Time!" (Where have you heard that before?)

Here's an example of the concept that "the person with the money calls the shots." You go to a restaurant. The hostess directs you to the nearest table that happens to be adjacent to a family with noisy kids. You are the person with the money. You do not have to sit there just because the hostess either hasn't thought much about your comfort or chose the table because it was closer for the server. You point to another table and say you want that one. You will get it, usually without question. If a question is raised about why you want another table, ask the hostess whether the food is free. If the answer is that you must pay for the food today as on any other day, say that since you are paying you want the other table. The person having the money calls the shots. Remember that principle, when you are the person with the money and also when you provide the product and want the money.

Interrelations of Various Business Areas

A business can be pictured as a mobile whose central part is attached to a ceiling or its balance plane that allows parts of the mobile to balance, as illustrated in Figure 1.1. An example, found in some homes, is a mobile shaped like a ship; smaller ships hang from it on different lengths of line and the device is suspended from above. When one of the small ships is hit or displaced, the entire mobile moves in an attempt to establish equilibrium. If one of the suspended items was subjected to a major change, for example, a weight was added to one small ship, the entire mobile would shift position to attain equilibrium. A business operates the same way. If a major change is made in any one area, the other areas must adapt to attain equilibrium.

For example, if a research and development group designs a new product, marketing and sales must make suitable changes in their activities, quality control procedures must be designed for the new product, and the manufacturing facility must be geared up to produce the item. This situation occurs in many areas of life. Every individual's life includes aspects such as career, social, and religious activities. When a major displacement occurs in any aspect of life, the other factors will shift to achieve equilibrium. Unplanned

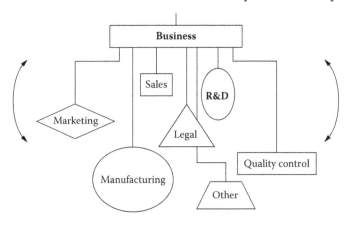

Figure 1.1   Mobile as business model.

unemployment is a good example. Other activities of life will adjust accordingly. The person may pray more or less. Socially, he may be more restrained or become more social in an effort to ease the burden of unemployment.

If a major item of equipment is purchased for any department of a business, employees must be trained to operate the equipment and/or more employees may have to be hired. Again, a shifting of components takes place, i.e., people within a department, to return the operation to equilibrium status. On a global basis, a major change such as a shortage of oil from a particular country will cause the economies of many other countries to adapt to compensate for the shortage and attempt to return to their equilibrium states.

A manager in business must direct his own area, but at the same time realize that his area must maintain relations with other areas. Continuous interfacing occurs among areas such as research and development, manufacturing, marketing, sales, quality control, and others, as already noted. The higher up a manager is, the more important are relationships with other areas because the ramifications are greater.

An interesting dynamic occurs when a large change occurs in one area. The other areas will relate to that change in such a way as to attain an equilibrium situation; however, while this is always attempted, it is never achieved. The reason for this is because just as equilibrium is nearly reached, the business must shift to higher goals, again disrupting the shift toward equilibrium. This is the way it should be. When people achieve particular goals, for example, a job promotion, they work to perform at that level but immediately set the next higher goal which is another promotion in the future, and then work toward that higher goal.

Whenever management sees that a goal is achieved, for example, a particular market share or level of sales volume is reached (or nearly reached), new products or new applications of existing products are designed to increase sales further. Money may have to be borrowed to facilitate a plant expansion, and equilibrium will be sought again but is never really reached. A firm that reaches equilibrium will not be looking forward. Thus the apparent paradox is, in reality, a desired quality in business.

Forms of Business Organization

There are three primary forms of business organization: the sole proprietorship, the partnership, and the corporation. It is important to know the differences among these three forms and their advantages and disadvantages. Many businesses start as partnerships and then transform into corporations when it is determined beneficial for the firm. Some business are created as corporations; some are sole proprietorships and remain that way. All three types will be discussed.

Sole Proprietorship

A sole proprietorship is a business owned by a single person. It is easy to set up. In effect, a person simply starts doing business. It is in reality, a little more complicated. Many cities and states require licenses to do business even for a sole proprietorship. Of course, a business person would want to purchase insurance policies to cover such matters as disability. While it would not be very smart to do business without vital insurance coverage, it is not a requirement to do business. This section focuses on the requirements for doing business.

A sole proprietorship presents significant advantages; for example this type of ownership is relatively easy and inexpensive to form. No formal charter for operations is required, and sole proprietorships are usually subjected to fewer government regulations than larger businesses such as corporations. Sole proprietorships do not pay corporate income taxes that are usually at higher rates than individual taxes; the earnings of the firm are subject only to personal income taxes. As with a corporation, earnings that are reinvested in the business result in a tax deduction. Business expenses for sole proprietors are deducted from gross income to yield net income. The individual proprietor determines how much to reinvest in a business he alone owns.

A sole proprietorship presents certain limitations. Since the business is relatively small and is owned by a single individual, it is difficult to obtain large amounts of capital for expansion or other purposes. It is also unusual for a proprietorship to undergo a major expansion such as doubling or tripling in size. If this occurs, the sole proprietor might consider establishing an alternative form of business such as a corporation. Additionally, a proprietor has *unlimited personal liability* for the business and he can lose assets beyond those owned by the company, for example, a car, house, or boat if a significant debt is incurred or if the business is sued. In reality the nature of a business determines the probability of such a lawsuit to some extent. The possibility is remote for a business that manufactures or sells shoes. However, in businesses such as food establishments, where a person can claim he was poisoned by the food or slipped on a banana peel and sustained serious injury, the probability increases.

The life of the proprietorship is limited to the life of the individual who started it. This means the business will cease to exist when the owner dies. The assets will be divided among debtors, the government, and the heirs. An heir or other individual may immediately restart the business and the public will assume the same business is continuing. Legally and in reality, the original business dissolved and a new proprietorship or other form of business was created.

Some businesses start as proprietorships and then change to corporate form when growth causes the disadvantages of the sole proprietorship to outweigh the advantages. Many firms convert to corporate structures despite the higher tax rate, because of significant individual tax deductions and other associated benefits.

Partnership

A partnership is similar to a proprietorship except that it is a business, usually unincorporated, owned by two or more persons. The advantages and disadvantages are the same ones that apply to a sole proprietorship. A partnership is easy to form; two or more people simply decide to form a partnership. That partnership does not pay corporate income taxes. The individual partners are taxed on the income they receive from the business, distributed proportionately as they previously agreed, as personal income. The partnership has similar disadvantages to a proprietorship—the most important of which is unlimited personal liability. Note here that if two partners in a business encounter a major problem and one partner disappears for any reason (for example, going to a foreign country, whereabouts unknown), the courts will find the remaining partner responsible for all of the debt of the partnership. Essentially, the courts locate any partners they can find and make them pay. If you are a partner in a business, keep close track of the whereabouts of your partners and their activities. If one partner starts purchasing exotic vacations, boats, and other luxuries in the name of the business, you may be responsible for paying for the luxuries. (There's more about partners in Chapter 19.)

A partnership organization also has a limited life. If a partner dies, the partnership ceases to exist. Again, as with a sole proprietorship, a new business can immediately be formed—a new partnership composed of the remaining partners, or any restructuring they choose. As far as the general public is concerned, the business continues, even though in a legal sense the partnership ceased and a new one was created. Another issue is the difficulty of transferring ownership. The more partners that are involved, the more difficult it is to get them to agree on anything.

The tax treatment is very similar to that of a proprietorship. An important point to remember is that the profits of a partnership consisting of two persons are not necessarily divided into 50% shares for each partner. In a partnership involving three persons, the profits are not necessarily divided into 33% portions. Profits are divided in a manner that is agreed upon at the beginning of the partnership, usually in proportion to the amount of money invested by each individual, but other formulas may apply, for example, the number of hours worked each week by the partners. One may work 60 hours a week and another may work 30 hours a week and these figures come into play in determining the returns to the partners. It is imperative to have an attorney prepare partnership papers; all partners should sign them in the presence of the attorney before starting the business. Trust is easier to maintain when legal documents are involved.

Corporation

A corporation is a distinct legal entity created by a state. It is separate and distinct from its owners and managers; its life is unlimited. The separate and distinct nature of a corporation gives it major advantages. For example, its life may continue long after the original owners are deceased or leave the organization for any reason. Ownership can be transferred easily because it is represented by shares of stock that are transferred far more easily than ownership interests in a partnership or a proprietorship. Ownership of a corporation is subject to limited liability. If you purchase $5,000 worth of stock of a corporation that

	Sole Proprietorship	Partnership	Corporation
Formation	Easy	Easy	Some Effort
Raise Significant Capital	Difficult	Difficult	Easy
Liability	Unlimited	Unlimited	Limited
Life	As the Proprietor's	As the Partners'	Continuous
Taxes	As Personal Income	As Personal Income	Higher Rates as a Corporation

Figure 1.2 Comparison of three forms of business.

faces financial problems and owes huge amounts of money to creditors, the maximum amount you can lose is your initial $5,000 investment. The corporation, as a legal entity, is responsible for the entire debt. If it cannot pay its debts, it declares bankruptcy. The owner of a proprietorship would be responsible for all the business debts incurred and would have to use personal assets to pay them. In a partnership, a partner with assets would be held liable for debts if his partners could not pay their portions. As a firm grows larger, the benefit of limited liability alone is a worthwhile reason to consider incorporating.

The concept of double taxation is associated with corporate earnings. In society today, we often pay taxes on income several times over, for example, by using already taxed income to purchase theater tickets whose cost includes an amusement tax. Double taxation involves taxation of the earnings of a corporation before dividends are distributed. After dividends are distributed to the shareholders, they are taxed as income of the shareholders. Figure 1.2 compares the three forms of business organization.

Some Variations

There are some variations of business organization. The first concerns partnerships. A limited partnership consists of one or more general partners and several limited partners. The general partner or partners usually make the decisions for the partnership and in all the other respects have more to gain and lose. The limited partners invest money but cannot lose any more than they invest. Their returns are also limited. A general partner who actively manages the business is going to earn a greater return on investment than a limited partner. Limited partners usually have nothing to say about the direction of the business or the decisions made. Usually, the general partner has the greater responsibilities, makes the decisions, and has more to gain. Usually, facts about the business or investment are presented to individuals who may decide to become limited partners. If they decide positively, they invest money in the hope of obtaining a reasonably good return if the partnership is successful.

A person with a great deal of knowledge about a particular field or project and who had some money available, but not enough to fund a business, might consider a limited partnership. This arrangement would, in effect, allow him to recruit partners who would put up the money and let the general partner with the expertise run the organization. Of course, as with all good business deals, all the details would be set forth in writing at the time of formation.

Another variation is a Subchapter S corporation, so named because this type of organization is authorized under Subchapter S of the Internal Revenue Service (IRS) Code. Subchapter S allows a smaller business to incorporate to limit the liability of the organization and encourage investments by shareholders. The IRS limits the number of shareholders to 35 or fewer. The primary advantage is that the income is taxed as personal income, which for a smaller business, will usually result in a lower rate than the corporate tax rate. Therefore, a Subchapter S corporation enjoys the limited liability of a corporation and usually a lower tax rate. The regular corporate structure that was described earlier in this chapter, and that is usually considered when talking of corporations, by the way, is a Subchapter C corporation.

Current Trends

A recent trend is that companies are merging or are purchased by other companies. Something else is also occurring more frequently and may not be beneficial if you are a consumer of a firm's products. Investment firms are purchasing technology or science-based companies and installing new CEOs who know little about the nature or quality of the products involved. The purpose of this technique is to increase profits over the short term and then sell the firm in a few years. This involves selling assets and closing plants. The new CEO's purpose is to make the company look good so it can be sold.

How do you know that this has happened? There are two indications. First, you can investigate the ownership on the stock exchange records. You can also read an interview with the CEO or better yet, see and hear an interview. You'll have an answer within five minutes. When asked about the company, the CEO will either stress the stock price and say nothing about the quality (because he or she doesn't know or care), or the CEO will talk about quality. Obviously, quality is the most important factor because consumers want to purchase products of a company that focuses on quality. A company that focuses on stock price may produce inferior products and provide poor or non-existent customer service. A CEO who discusses quality probably represents a company that has excellent quality and customer service. Such sales have occurred in the pharmaceutical industry and led to the downfall of some firms but the enrichment of participating CEOs. We're talking about product quality here; price is an entirely separate issue.

Goals of a Business

Most finance and other business textbooks define the goal of a corporation as "maximizing shareholder wealth." This means maximizing the value of the common stock held by stockholders. Corporation managers usually hold significant amounts of stock in the companies that employ them. In fact, stock bonuses are common incentives for recruiting and retaining top management personnel. (There's more to be said about bonuses in Chapter 17.)

The question of whether a stock price is maximized can always be raised. For example, if a company's stock sold at $18 per share and was selling at $25 per share a year later, any stockholder could always inquire whether more effort or productivity could have increased the stock price to $26 or $30 or more. Determining the maximized price of a stock is very difficult. Usually, reasonable gains are satisfactory to stockholders.

Partnerships and proprietorships do not issue stock. The owner's or partners' equity is equivalent to shareholder wealth. Actually, for any kind of business, whether ownership is called owners' equity or shareholders' wealth, the net profit is the true "bottom line." Business owners and managers always try to maximize profits. In a very simplistic form, the accounting equation defines the situation:

$$\text{Assets} - \text{Liabilities} = \text{Equity}$$

The equation is obvious but it clearly makes the point whether the business is a corner delicatessen or Exxon Corporation. The assets minus the liabilities equal the equity or net worth of a company. You can apply this equation to your own situation. Total the values of all assets you own including your house, car, and other property. Subtract from that the total of all your debts. The remainder is what you really own—your equity or net worth.

Company Philosophies

Companies have philosophies just like individuals have philosophies or styles. Figure 1.3 illustrates a typical company setup. The shareholders of a corporation elect the board of directors. The board of directors (more will be said about the board below) hires the chief executive officer (CEO) and he or she reports to the board. In turn, the president reports to the CEO, and the various vice presidents report to the president. In a smaller corporation, one person may serve as both president and CEO and the corporation may not need vice presidents. The number and type of executive positions depend on the size of the corporation.

In a partnership, sometimes two or more partners act as president and CEO, but more commonly one partner will function as president and CEO and another will function as vice president, treasurer, and secretary.

In a sole proprietorship, the proprietor handles everything. It's that simple. He may not have the CEO or president title, but in effect he does every task. He does not report to any other person and has authority to make all decisions. He also serves as the board of directors, CEO, president, and all the other decision makers.

A company's philosophy means that the CEO will follow certain practices such as taking or avoiding risks, imposing greater or lesser emphasis on research and development, and operating secretively or

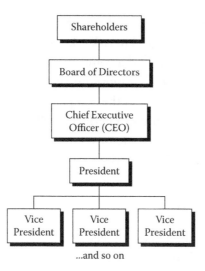

Figure 1.3 Company organization chart.

openly. The president and the vice presidents will reflect philosophies similar to those of the CEO. Since the vice presidents report to the president, who in turn reports to the CEO, they will exhibit similar philosophies. If they do not, their tenures will be short. Theoretically, the CEO reflects the philosophy of the company. As an example, if a CEO, as a reflection of the board of directors and therefore the company, is prone to avoid risks (as many are), this characteristic will be exhibited by top management. In this case, a department head who takes risks is philosophically different from the company as reflected by top management. Sooner or later the department head or the top management will have to go. More often than not, the department head will go even if he is an exceptionally talented individual. If his philosophy or style is significantly different from that of the company and its management, the affected individual will feel more comfortable and advance his career elsewhere; that will not happen in a company whose philosophy differs from his.

Adhering to company philosophy is not a matter of equal opportunity for all. It's common sense. Top management wants only managers who think as they do. If your style is drastically different, as illustrated above, you will be at odds with top management. Why should they continue to employ you? If someone must go, it will usually be the person with a different philosophy. Recognize this early and if you can't find a way to change top management, determine what your style is with regard to risk taking, openness versus secrecy, and other qualities. Then find a company that has that same philosophy—where you can readily move up the line. Why? Because you exhibit the same philosophy as the company. Assuming you have the fundamental talents required to perform well, you are now part of a company that treats you as one of its own. It not only makes good sense—it's the way business works.

Relatives in a Business

Some businesses employ staffs of relatives and close friends. If you are employed by a small business (sales below $20 million per year) and relatives such as fathers and children work there, you should get out even faster than when you have a different philosophy. If the family needs you, you will be favored as long as the need exists. Always remember that "blood is thicker than water."

This is a fact. Many presidents have been heard to say something to the effect of, "That guy's a real foul-up, but he's my sister's kid. I have to leave him heading the division, even if he's running it into the ground."

Remember, you may be extremely talented, but the relatives see each other at family dinners and social events, etc. You are simply a person in their employ. Here again, recognize the situation and find a firm where you're appreciated and can move up as rapidly as you feel you should.

Planning

Planning is a vital aspect of any business and will be discussed throughout this book in different settings. Put simply, "If you don't know where you're going, how will you ever know if you got there?" While various texts list different numbers of elements in a plan, sometimes as many as ten, there are really only five. Here are Farley's five planning steps:

- Decide where you want to go or what you want to do.
- Determine what it will take to get there or pursue what you want to do.

- Make the decision.
- Do it! (sometimes called the *implementing* step).
- Follow up. Seek feedback (also called the *monitoring* step).

As a simple example, assume you want to take a ride in a boat. You have to determine where you want to go. After that, you look on the charts and determine the distance, how much fuel and food you'll need, and what else is required. Then you decide to take the trip or not to take the trip.

Some decisions take one millisecond; others can take a long, long time, depending on the process you follow and how fast you make decisions. The next step is *do it!* Get in the boat and start the trip. The last step is monitoring. In our example, look at where you're going because the wind, ocean currents, and tides—even if calculated carefully—may have thrown you off course. Now, comes an important point. If you are off course, before you make an immediate correction, look at where you're going. Maybe the port that you're heading for is better than the one you planned to visit. If you then decide to go to the better port, reset your course toward it. This means you have to recalculate fuel, food, and other factors and determine whether your supplies are sufficient or you have to obtain more supplies. On the other hand, if your decision is to head for the original port, make sure you have enough supplies on board that will enable you to complete the trip as planned.

This analogy of a boat trip, perhaps a distance of only a few miles, clearly illustrates the planning goals of a business such as determining market share, introducing new products, and increasing sales and profits. Again, whether the business is a small neighborhood delicatessen or a Fortune 500 corporation, the planning process involves the same elements. And remember that you must know where you're going before you set out on a trip in the business world.

2
MARKETING

The marketing function encompasses many aspects. Some people use the terms *sales* and *marketing* interchangeably. Actually they are very different activities. Sales is "only" one of the activities accomplished by the marketing function, but a very important one. It is so important that the owner of a company who wants to hire one person to help his company grow should hire a salesperson. This is based on the premise that you already have the first requirement—your product. The next step is to find people who will sell the product. Sales is the subject of the next chapter, but it is important to distinguish the marketing from sales functions.

There are numerous definitions of Marketing. They all center around "The process by which products and services are introduced to the marketplace." This is a rather broad definition. Marketing is, essentially, identifying what the customer wants and needs, and performing activities such as advertising and sales to bring your product to the customer.

We will now discuss marketing functions:

- Marketing research
- Customers
- Differential advantage
- Consumer demographics
- Consumer decision process
- Cognitive dissonance
- Product life cycle
- Principle of reverse effect

Marketing Research

This specialized type of research not only involves learning what your potential customers want, but includes much more. You must know what's going on with the economy and be knowledgeable about your competition. Your product is only a single item in this research scenario. You must be able to answer several questions. What is the current state of the economy? Is it such that people will purchase my product at this time? Who is my competition? Do my competitors offer a better product in some way? Does the customer believe he needs my product? Can I make the customer believe he needs my product? Can I make the customer believe this to the extent that he will purchase the product? What must I do to make sure the customer purchases my product instead of a competitor's?

Surveys play a large role in marketing research. However, you must realize that people do not always do what they say they'll do. For example, surveys are often taken in shopping malls. A typical question is: "Would you buy the following product…?" Most people answer that they will, and then buy a competitor's product when they see that it may be priced lower or is packaged attractively to catch attention. Remember that what people say they will do is not always what they do; in fact, they seldom do what they say they will do. And your customers include those people.

Another thing to remember about surveys is that the results are skewed from the very start. Not everyone responds to surveys. Think, for example, of surveys conducted in a shopping mall where a person stops you and asks you to answer a few questions. Only certain individuals will stop and respond; others simply don't care to spend the time. Therefore, the survey is skewed because it represents the opinions only of those people who were willing to stop shopping and render opinions. This skewed distribution may or may not be non-representative of the entire population; participation is something to take into consideration. The same reasoning applies to surveys obtained through regular mail and e-mail.

Another thing to remember is that surveys are usually conducted by a third party firm that specializes in customer surveys. Often the respondent (you) is not given an opportunity to express an opinion about any aspect of the subject in his own words. Discussion-type answers must be read carefully and interpreted, and that costs money. The answers are preset in multiple choice format; major issues are frequently not covered, usually for cost saving purposes. It is very expensive to conduct a survey that will provide the most accurate results, so some companies elect to take the less expensive (cheap) route and thus the results have less reliability.

Test marketing—putting your product in the marketplace where you can see and monitor customer purchasing behavior—is a preferred method. It allows you to see what customers actually choose. It will cost you a bit more money to run a market test than to run a survey, but your results will be more accurate and you can predict your market better.

Customers

A customer purchases an item in the belief that he or she needs it. The key term is "perceived need." For example, if you manufacture VCRs and you have data to indicate that almost every household has a VCR, how will you sell more of your product?

You can make people believe that every household should have two VCRs. This is especially true for households that own two or more television sets. If you can convince people that they may want to record two shows that are broadcast at the same time, you can demonstrate a "need" for a second VCR. After you convince the customer of the need, you have to show him why he should buy your VCR instead of someone else's. What you think about the need for two VCRs in a household is incidental. What the customer thinks (or what you can make the customer think) is the important issue.

Differential Advantage

The reason people should buy your product instead of a competitor's— after they decide to buy somebody's product—is going to be the result of your differential advantage. Why should they buy your product instead of your competitor's? Why is your product better for them than your competitor's? Do you have:

- Lower prices?
- Better guarantee?
- More durable product?
- Better customer service, perhaps an 800 number for customer calls?

What is your differential advantage? It is the reason for people to buy your product in preference to your competitor's after they have made the decision to buy the product.

Consumer Demographics

Consumer demographic information allows you to *target* your market. The two major categories of marketing are *mass marketing* and *target marketing*. If you are selling newspapers, you can put them in vending boxes on any street corner and probably sell them all. This is mass marketing. If, on the other hand, you are selling expensive cars, such as BMWs, you want to make a good choice of location for your dealership and determine the best way to advertise. You are certainly not going to put your dealership in an economically distressed area or advertise your automobiles in magazines that are read mostly by low income families. On the contrary, you will place your dealership in an affluent section of a city or suburb with high income population and advertise in magazines read by people whose incomes enable them to purchase BMWs. This is known as target marketing and it is based on utilizing consumer demographics. The list of demographics below applies to a typical BMW purchaser* and is used here as an illustration:

- Age of consumer? (for example, 30 to 55 years old)
- Annual income of consumer? (for example, $50,000 to $150,000)
- Percentage self-employed and percentage employed by corporations?
- Type of geographic area where their businesses are conducted?
- Type of geographic area where they reside?

Many types of demographic studies may be performed. Be careful not to be overwhelmed with data, some of which may be useless. For example, you may obtain—at a significant price—data on the height or range of heights of typical BMW owners, but is that really significant? It doesn't matter how many BMW owners are 6 feet tall (although that may be of interest to car designers). Height will probably have nothing to do with their purchase decisions, but you likely can find someone who gathered this information and will sell it to you.

You may obtain data on whether potential customers are college graduates. That may or may not be significant. The key point here is that when you gather data to compile a demographic profile of your

---

* The items on the list are not necessarily those used by the Bavarian Motor Works, manufacturer of BMW automobiles.

consumers, you're investing time and money to obtain information. Pause and think about what characteristics are required for a profile of your typical customer or consumer. (The customer purchases the product and the consumer uses it. In this context, the terms are used interchangeably. More about this later.) Obtain the information you need for target marketing but don't spend extra time and money accumulating a lot of statistics you don't need.

Consumer Decision Process

It is distinctly to your advantage to know the steps in the consumer decision process shown in Figure 2.1:

- Stimulus
- Problem awareness
- Information search
- Evaluation of alternatives
- Purchase
- Postpurchase behavior

Stimulus triggers the decision process. It may be the recommendation of a friend or something that you've seen in a newspaper ad or on a television commercial.

In *problem awareness,* the customer realizes that your product may solve a problem or satisfy an unfulfilled desire. For example, a customer may see your advertisement for a suit, realize that some of his suits are wearing out, and purchase a suit from you. That would solve his problem of having older worn-out suits.

The *information search* stage involves information gathering by the customer to determine the various products available to solve his

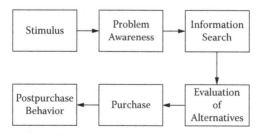

Figure 2.1 Consumer decision process.

important problems and analyzing the advantages and disadvantages of each product. In other words, the customer is searching for alternatives before locking in on your product.

The customer then moves to the *evaluation of alternatives* stage. In his own way, by whatever comparative mechanism he selects, he will evaluate the available alternatives.

The next step is the *purchase*. After the customer selects the best alternative, the decision to buy is made. (Some marketing experts consider the decision as a separate step; here we consider the decision to purchase and the purchase as a single step.) The purchase may be made over the phone, via mail, over the Internet, directly with you or your agent, or by any number of ways.

There is a nebulous situation that occurs when someone tells you he will buy your product but doesn't make a down payment on the purchase. Is this transaction a purchase or not? The choice is yours. It depends on your policies, how well you know the customer, what risks you're willing to take, and various other factors. As a general guideline, you're the marketer. Decide what makes you feel comfortable. If getting some money up front in the form of cash or a credit card makes you feel more comfortable than not getting it, count the monetary transaction as a purchase.

In the *postpurchase behavior* stage, the customer may no longer experience the good feeling he had after making the decision to buy and concluding the purchase and may now feel some regret. This is a psychological tendency. The customer had good feelings about the purchase for several hours or even days, and now questions whether he made the right choice or should have spent "that much money." These may be strong feelings based on the amount of money involved and its value in the mind of the customer. A multimillionaire may not have strong regrets after purchasing a $100,000 automobile, whereas a person earning $30,000 or less annually may suffer serious second thoughts after purchasing a $17,000 compact car. This is an important feeling on the part of every customer and must be considered (and will be in the next section). For now, remember the steps of consumer decision making and know where you and your customer are at each point along the way.

Cognitive Dissonance

While postpurchase behavior of a customer may involve telling other people good news about your product, it frequently involves *cognitive dissonance*. This is a strong psychological feeling on the part of a customer and must be handled effectively. How? You take the active step and follow up. For example, if someone buys a washing machine from you, send the customer a free box of detergent or a coupon for free detergent a few days after the washing machine is delivered. In the case of an automobile, call the customer and ask how he or she likes the car. Some marketers claim these calls cause customers to raise questions. A customer who doesn't like your product will call you. If you believe in your product and want the customer satisfied now, and want that customer to return, you want referrals to other customers. That makes the calls certainly worth the time and effort. You can probably think of many ways to follow up with customers, depending on your product and the needs of your customers.

Product Life Cycle

Figure 2.2 depicts a typical product life cycle. The graph plots dollars versus time. Sales begin slowly at the introduction stage. The next stage is growth and, as the name implies, the number of sales

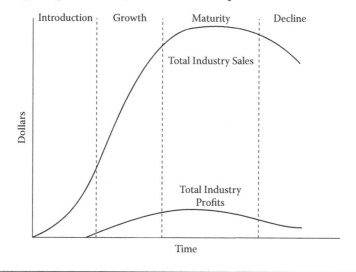

Figure 2.2 Typical product life cycle.

is increasing rapidly. At the maturity stage, sales continue increasing slowly but essentially "level out." This would not be bad if they continued at that level, but the final stage is decline—when sales decrease and continue downward. The curve representing profit in the figure shows a time lag between sales and the realization of profit. One key factor of the product life cycle is that a seller doesn't always know the time frame involved in the cycle when he brings a product to the market. In fact, he seldom knows.

Manual typewriters are no longer manufactured, and therefore no new ones are sold. The life cycle graph for a manual typewriter would indicate that this product has completed its decline stage and no longer exists as a newly manufactured item. On the other hand, you can draw separate graphs for electric typewriters, electronic typewriters, word processors, and computers with word processing programs. If you want to draw a plot of the typewriter product and your definition includes *all* modern typewriters including computers and word processors, the chart will reveal that the product is in the growth stage. The point is that you can draw a chart representative of your product as you define it.

Figure 2.3 shows other types of product life cycles. A classic is a product that has achieved a high level and continues at that level. If you examine the life cycle of a fad, for example a fashion design expected to have a short cycle, you will note a rapid rise to the maximum and then a rapid decrease, after which a new design is introduced.

If you know where you are in the life cycle of your product, you can find ways to "stretch it out" at the maturity stage or design another product that grows as the earlier product declines.

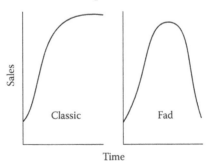

Figure 2.3 Other types of life cycles.

Remember, you can draw various life cycle curves, each for a different definition of a product. That is, if you use different degrees of specificity, you can compile different life cycles. For example, the life cycle of the automobile has not hit the maturity stage yet. However, many types of automobiles are no longer produced. They reached their decline stages and some of the companies that produced them have gone out of the business. Everything has a life cycle. Plants do, animals do, you and I do. Of course, we hope our life cycles are very long ones. You also hope that your product has a very long life cycle.

Principle of Reverse Effect

It's very important today…more than ever…to discuss the principle of reverse effect. It represents a road you do not want to travel. We see examples every day and the principle is practiced by alleged marketing professionals who really don't know what they're doing.

Let's start by defining the principle: There is an optimum amount of marketing, advertising, or solicitation that can be done to promote an item before potential customers are turned off and driven away—to not purchase the product or to purchase it from a competitor.

Persistence is good. Being a nuisance is not good. In marketing, the big difference between persistence and nuisance is that a good marketer is persistent and an inept marketer goes beyond persistence to the point of becoming a nuisance. We'll look at some examples and how to cope with them. Observe the graph labeled the "Principle of Reverse Effect" (Figure 2.4). Let's use ordinary jeans as an example of the principle. Initially priced at $10 (although it's questionable whether the seller could sell at this price without taking a loss), no buyer thinks that jeans can be worth anything because the price is too low to convey quality. As the price of jeans increases, customers begin to perceive quality in line with what they expect a good pair of jeans would cost. At a $40 price, more customers perceive quality and therefore buy the jeans. In our case, this continues until the price of $60 is reached.

If the $60 price is increased, some potential buyers may think the jeans are overpriced and will not buy them (at least not in that store). As the price increases further, more potential buyers will consider the jeans overpriced and not buy them. This is the principle of reverse effect.

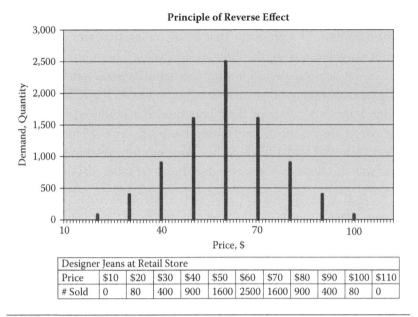

Figure 2.4 Principle of reverse effect.

In reality, the effect is not as symmetrical as the effect shown in the figure. It can rise or decrease sharply. For example, perhaps only 100 pairs were sold at $80; that's significantly different from the 900 pairs shown in the symmetrical chart. The key issue here is recognizing the point beyond which the desired result is reversed. Not only not reached, but reversed! You can sometimes predict that point; you simply have to be watchful and realize when you have reached it. The shape of a price-versus-demand chart for any item depends on how necessary consumers think it is.

Several years ago a town decided to increase its merchant tax from 6 to 7% in the belief that the town would collect more money. What the town officials didn't consider was that the merchants were already tired of paying the 6% tax and when the 7% was instituted, several moved their businesses to the suburbs, leaving the town with a higher tax rate but less income from taxes collected. The town also had several vacant buildings with no new businesses interested in moving into them. The town ultimately reduced the tax rate but had to convince businesses to start up or relocate there. The significant point is that at no time in its brief existence did the 7% rate yield more revenue than the 6% rate. The principle of reverse effect came into play.

In another example, the federal government several years ago decided to raise the tax on luxury yachts from 6 to 10% in the belief that it would generate more revenue. The federal officials didn't realize that people who bought such boats wouldn't stand for that. The government knew that yacht buyers were wealthy and paid cash and therefore assumed that the government could make more money by increasing the tax. The government didn't realize that those customers wouldn't be "pushed around." The yacht owners kept their existing boats instead of buying new ones. Not only did the government not get the revenue expected, but the boat dealerships, because of slower sales, had to lay off employees. The principle of reverse effect decided the issue.

While you want to maximize your profit, you should be aware that if your efforts reach the principle of reverse effect, you will lose business and probably have to exert considerable effort to regain buyers' trust. Let's consider some examples of the reverse effect principle in marketing.

Example 1—Internet e-mails about a company's sales. Sending an e-mail once in a while can be good. A daily e-mail from a company begins to interfere with your work and your other Internet activities, and therefore becomes disruptive. You may determine that you will not buy from that company because its advertising reached the point of annoyance.

Example 2—Telephone and mail solicitations from charitable organizations. Such organizations are fundamentally good, but they may contract fund raising to a third party that may charge a percentage of funds received. Some organizations may call or e-mail you several times a week. For many people that crosses the line from marketing to annoyance and the result is that their money goes to other charities that don't solicit repeatedly.

Example 3—Before you can log on to access your bank account via the Internet, you are exposed to advertisements for new bank programs. You don't want this. You simply want to access your account. Your bank didn't know when to stop advertising so you could conduct your business. You may decide to change banks.

Example 4—Movie theater previews before the main feature. You must pay for your ticket before entering the theatre and will be subjected to previews of movies in a genre that does not interest you. The previews run a total of 25 minutes and delay the 100-minute main feature. You decide to wait and purchase the DVD that may include previews, but you can bypass them with the "menu" button.

In all the cases presented above, marketing people didn't know when to stop. Allowing marketing efforts to reach the principle of reverse effect is amateurish and counterproductive. Know when a seller crosses the line from persistence to the principle of reverse effect. Don't operate according to the principle and don't accept such efforts as a consumer. When you are exposed to such tactics, tell others so that they do not patronize companies that use these tactics. The companies may change their tactics after they see sales drop or ultimately go out of business. They will, of course, blame the economy and not their ignorance of how to treat customers, but that's another story.

Marketing Your Talents

One other area to which you might apply the contents of this chapter is using the principles of marketing in your career. Marketing does not apply only to products. You can market your talents. In reality, we market ourselves and our opinions many times every day. In your career progression you can use these marketing principles to your advantage with your employer.

Ask yourself, "How can I market my talents to my employer and increase my employer's perceived need of me?" If you can answer that and act on your answer, your career can be much more successful.

3
SALES

The sales function involves direct contacts with customers. That fact alone makes sales very important because customers represent the lifeblood of your business. As noted earlier, the first person who should be hired after a product is designed is a salesperson to generate business.

Keep in mind that sales brings in money; other areas spend it!

Many years ago, after the Industrial Revolution came about, people stopped making what they needed. People who made their own clothes could then go to stores to buy them. The same situation applied to canning and preserving foods. Stores sold many manufactured items and demand was so great that people flocked to stores to make the purchases. Keep the word "demand" in mind. It's an important part of the supply-and-demand function that's a key facet of business.

As the years passed, more products became available and their popularity increased. In fact, for many, shopping became fun. The sales function then consisted mainly of notifying customers about what products you had and where those products could be purchased. Today, we find tremendous numbers of products available in a market of intense competition. Think about the large number of products now available that couldn't be purchased as recently as 20 years ago, for example, GPS units to aid automobile travel, "smart" phones with Internet access, and more. How does this explosion of products change sales activities? You have to tell the customers what you have, show them why they need it, and then convince them to purchase your product instead of others on the market. Didn't we say that about marketing in the previous chapter? Sure we did. Remember, sales is an integral part of marketing. This chapter on sales will cover:

- Who should be a salesperson? Where are such people?
- What are the characteristics of a successful salesperson?
- Who are your customers?

- Where are your customers?
- How do industrial and general sales differ?
- Does your company sell "business to business" or retail?
- How are salespersons compensated?
- Is segmentation territorial or by product?
- What is a sales forecast?
- What is the function of a sales manager?

Who Should Be a Salesperson? Where Are Such People?

The answers are everyone and everywhere. Certain persons carry the title and have the responsibility of selling products. These are the ones we usually say are "in sales" and are described in books about sales and marketing. In this chapter we will concentrate on people employed to sell. In reality, in business and in life, we are all salespersons all the time.

At a meeting, when you want to convince others to see your point of view, you're selling. When you want to go to a ball game and another person wants to attend the opera and you try to persuade that person to go to the ball game, you're selling. When you try to tell a policeman that you didn't mean to speed, you're selling. When you tell a potential employer that you should be hired, you're selling. Whenever you try to convince others to do as you want, you are selling your ideas, and you will be most effective if you use the principles and techniques that sales professionals use.

What Are the Characteristics of a Successful Salesperson?

This concept has been a subject of speculation and wonder for many years. If you can successfully categorize or (remember marketing terminology) define the demographic profile of a very successful salesperson, you can search, find, and hire one. And your company can make a lot of money. Many factors such as education and sociability can be considered, but certain abilities really count:

High level of product knowledge—This is obvious. A salesperson does not have to be the engineer who designed the product. He or she must be able to describe the important points of a product to a customer.

Good planning ability—A good salesperson must plan an efficient schedule and determine how to handle each individual customer. No two people are identical. A salesperson may treat them equally but not necessarily identically.

Ability to listen well—Before a salesperson talks excessively about his product, he should listen to his prospect and ask a few questions like "How are the widgets that you're currently using performing?" Then listen to the answer. The statements made by the prospective customer will indicate his satisfaction or areas of dissatisfaction that indicate problems. If the salesperson and his product can solve these problems, he has gained a new customer. Of course, if this customer already buys from your company and experiences a problem, you had better solve it fast!

Pleasing personality and ability to get along with people—This is readily apparent. A belief that a potential customer is better off by purchasing your product—the certainty that selling the customer a product is helping him—will come across in a presentation and optimize the probability of a sale.

Who Are Your Customers?

We should begin by differentiating purchasers and consumers. Sometimes these terms are used interchangeably but they should not be. The purchaser actually purchases, or buys, your product. The consumer uses or "consumes" the product he or someone else bought. Most people buy things they use. However, if someone bought you a gift, that person was the purchaser and you were the consumer. Of course, when you buy a gift for someone, you become the purchaser and the recipient is the consumer. So who's the customer? The purchaser or the consumer? Your first answer may well be that the purchaser is the customer. In most cases, this is correct, but in some cases the consumer is the customer even though someone else made the purchase.

Here's an example. Most, or at least, a large number of men's ties are purchased by women. In some cases, a woman decided to buy a tie, made the selection, and completed the purchase. A man may have hinted strongly that he wanted a tie for his birthday and even mentioned what style. (You say that if he hinted that strongly he's not a gentleman! That's a separate subject.)

The same situation occurs in reverse with perfumes. A man is frequently the customer and the woman is the consumer. By now you have the idea that the purchaser and the consumer may be two people. Think about it for a minute! The customer that you want to convince is the decision maker or the person who influences the decision maker significantly enough to direct the decision. That's your potential customer.

Where Are Your Customers?

In its most simplistic form the answer is one of the following:

- They are already buying from you. Find a way to sell them more.
- They are buying from your competition. Find a way to get them away from the competition by presenting an advantage of your product over the competition's. The advantage may be a superior product, good customer service, or improved delivery.
- They are not buying. Find a way to interest them in buying your product.

After you determine where your customers are (in which situation described above), direct your sales and marketing efforts by targeting your market according to its demographic profile as described in Chapter 2. The easiest, most dependable, or best method is obtaining repeat sales from existing customers or getting referrals from them. Companies that deal with your competitor may not know about you (certainly your competitor is not going to tell them!). If they have a product source, they may not actively seek another. Maybe such companies simply need to know that you're "around." It's worth a try.

How Do Industrial and General Sales Differ?

Sales to other than individual consumers are called business-to-business (B to B) sales. By far, most transactions are B to B sales, i.e., the highest dollar volume arises from sales to organizational consumers.

Retail sales come to mind when most people think of sales: an individual goes into a store, talks with a salesperson at a counter, and makes a purchase. Another type of selling activity is a brokerage type of sale, for example, a sale of real estate. When you want to buy a house, you go to a real estate agent who acts as a broker between the seller and you (the purchaser). You have purchased a house from a seller but someone (probably the seller) paid the real estate salesperson (broker) a commission.

Let's discuss an example of B to B sales for an over-the-counter (OTC) pharmaceutical product, as illustrated in Figure 3.1. The product is a bottle of tablets.* Let's say the product is an antacid. The tablets are contained in a plastic bottle that also contains a wad of cotton. The bottle includes a plastic cap and a label is affixed to the outside of the bottle. The bottle is packaged inside a cardboard box. This group of items constitutes the antacid tablet product that you purchased. Let's consider who bought what from whom to produce the bottle you bought.

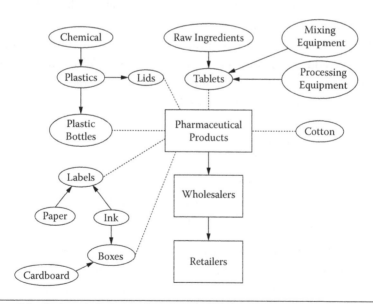

Figure 3.1   Business-to-business sales process for OTC pharmaceutical product.

---

* Pharmaceutical firms manufacture tablets; they don't "make pills." Do not refer to a pharmaceutical company as a "pill maker."

The tablets are manufactured by the pharmaceutical firm using chemicals it purchased from a supplier. Production people mixed the ingredients bought from an industrial supplier and may have contracted with a third party to mix the formulation. The third party compressed or manufactured the tablets on machinery purchased from another supplier. The tablets then traveled on a conveyor line from another industrial supplier before they were transferred into plastic bottles.

The bottles were purchased from another company that manufactured the bottles from materials it bought from a plastics supplier. The plastics supplier made the plastics from other raw materials purchased from a chemical supplier. The cotton was purchased from yet another company. The cap may have been purchased from the same company that sold the bottle or from another supplier. The label was purchased from a label manufacturer that bought paper and ink from one or more companies. The box was purchased from a supplier that printed the box using ink and cardboard bought from other manufacturers, using production equipment purchased from another company.

Hopefully, this example illustrates the number of sales transactions that take place to bring a product to the retail market. Wholesalers and distributors in the distribution chain between manufacturer and consumer add more transactions to the process. You can track this process for any number of retail products, for example, an air conditioner. The manufacturer purchased various metal parts from suppliers, then purchased the compressor from a company that manufactures compressors. The compressor company purchased refrigerants from a chemical company, and so on.

Other factors are involved in industrial sales. Some things to remember about the organizational consumer, that is, the company to which a salesperson is selling, include:

- Bidding and negotiations are relatively common practices.
- Specifications are set up for the product purchased; federal and state governments impose very rigid specifications.
- Industries acquire materials to use in their production steps, as shown in the examples above.
- Many companies have purchasing departments whose only function is purchasing required materials.

- Industrial sales should be based more on logic and less on emotion; the reverse is often true for retail sales.

If you sell industrial products and you want to find customers, you can utilize the Standard Industrial Classification Index. The federal government's Office of Management and Budget classifies businesses into numerical categories. This system, called the Standard Industrial Classification (SIC), categorizes major products and hence the companies that manufacture them by four digit code numbers (SIC codes). The first two digits of the SIC code show the major industrial group into which a company is classified. The code ranges for the ten divisions are:

CODE	INDUSTRIAL GROUP
01 to 09	Agriculture, forestry, and fishing
10 to 14	Mining
15 to 17	Construction
20 to 39	Manufacturing
40 to 49	Transportation, communication, electric, gas, and sanitary services
50 to 59	Wholesale and retail trade
60 to 67	Finance, insurance, and real estate
70 to 89	Services
91 to 97	Government
99	Nonclassifiable establishments

The third and fourth digits of the SIC code classify a company more specifically in its industry group. The SIC designation for the pharmaceutical company discussed earlier is 2834. The 28 represents a manufacturing company and the 3 and the 4 refer to specific types of manufacturing. The system is similar to the one used to categorize books in libraries. For example, the library assigns 500 series numbers to science books based on a numerical catalog system for all books. If you want to find a science book, go to the shelves that hold 500 series books. If you are looking for a chemistry book, go the 530 section; a physical chemistry book will have a 537 designation. The SIC system is very similar. It consists of a four-digit code that allows many variations.

Where do you find this information? In the reference section of a library. If you are not familiar with the reference section, reference librarians are among the most helpful people on earth. They like people and want to help. You will find, or be directed to the *Standard & Poor's Register of Corporations, Directors and Executives*. Other books provide similar information, but this register is a series of large books that list major companies. One volume lists companies numerically by SIC designation. Another lists companies alphabetically and provides information about corporate headquarters, officers' names, annual sales, type of business, and SIC designation.

If you see a company as a potential sales prospect, look up that company in the register, find its SIC, then refer to the volume listing SICs and you'll find names of all the other companies that manufacture the same product and may also be potential customers. Keep in mind that many large companies have several SIC numbers because they make a variety of products. Take the time to "zero in" on the companies that interest you. Instead of looking up only one company and finding a single SIC, you may note seven or eight numbers for a given company and may have to look up information about more companies to determine which number applies.

Many leading salespersons became leaders by visiting the library, talking to the reference librarian, and using information from *Standard & Poor's*. Then they actively pursued and called on these companies and achieved large sales volumes.

An alternative source of information is the Occupational Safety and Health Administration website www.osha.gov; look for "NAICS/SIC" (more about NAICS is presented below). Select NAICS or SIC and proceed with your search. Although we search the Internet for information and find it, reference librarians continue to perform valuable functions. At times they can direct you to the most expeditious route to information. They know the correct keywords to use to find information and thereby save your valuable time.

The SIC system was last updated in 1987. The North American Industry Classification System (NAICS) is newer. The following is from the NAICS website (www.naics.com):

"What is NAICS and how is it used? The North American Industry Classification System (NAICS, pronounced Nakes) was developed as the standard for use by Federal statistical agencies in classifying business establishments for the collection, analysis, and publication of statistical data related to the business economy of the U.S. NAICS was developed under the auspices of the Office of Management and Budget (OMB), and adopted in 1997 to replace the old Standard Industrial Classification (SIC) system. It was also developed in cooperation with the statistical agencies of Canada and Mexico to establish a 3-country standard that allows for a high level of comparability in business statistics among the three countries. NAICS is the first economic classification system to be constructed based on a single economic concept."

The SIC is still preferred by many who have used it over the years, and remains satisfactory for many uses, particularly for job hunting. Look for companies or types of companies that interest you, find their SIC codes, review companies with the same SIC, find out where they are located, the names of the officers, and address your inquiries accordingly. The same procedure applies if you choose to use the NAICS.

How Are Salespeople Compensated?

Companies have various ways of compensating sales staff. Compensation amounts vary from industry to industry and we would have to discuss wide ranges. We will, however, mention the various methods of compensating salespeople:

- Straight salary
- Commission only
- Salary plus commission

Straight Salary

The straight salary method is very direct. Compensation is not based on the amount of product or services sold. A salesperson who works for a company and is content to maintain existing accounts would be very satisfied on a straight salary basis. Sometimes this person is also expected to generate new accounts. "Inside" salespeople are usually paid straight salaries. This person is, in essence, an order taker (that's not meant to be disparaging; taking orders is a necessary function) who respond to phone calls as a customer service representative. This person knows how to take an order and check the status of orders. If a product is very technical, a customer may be turned over to a technical service representative who knows and handles technical issues and complex customer inquiries.

Commission Only

A very aggressive salesperson (aggressive in pursuing sales, not in personality) would rather work on commission and earn money for new business generated. This is the type of person who says, "I can make your business grow. I can get you new accounts and expand the existing ones." This person would probably not be content with a straight salary and may be paid commissions on recurring sales from accounts he generated.

Salary Plus Commission

The base salary plus commission is a combination that will provide a person with a base from which to meet ordinary living expenses. The commission may be added onto salary to compensate for new sales generated and/or existing sales maintained.

Which methods a company uses depend on its product line, its stage of growth, and its goals, especially for sales. Many companies pick one method and stick rigidly to it. There really is no reason, however, why a company can't devise combinations of these methods to reward salespersons as they progress with the company. You can start a person at a base salary and then, by agreement, change the arrangement to salary plus commission, lowering the base salary and intending that commissions will make up for the difference or exceed it. If you are running a sales department, pursue new ideas and determine what is best for salespersons in your company. Don't worry about what the other salespersons will say about one person who earns a lot of money through commissions. If they're that good, talk to them about switching to commissions so they can earn more.

Consider company-owned vehicles. A vehicle is worth several thousand dollars a year—equivalent to a salary. The benefit of driving a company car for personal use is worth thousands of dollars to a salesperson. This is no longer common because of liability and insurance considerations. It is simpler to restrict company cars to business use.

The key, as mentioned above, is to not restrict your thinking. Think creatively and set up a compensation structure in your company in accordance with your existing product line, your current sales, and your goals.

Is Segmentation Territorial or by Product?

This comparison is best made through an example. Let's say Charlie, Sally, and Ralph work in sales. Charlie sells product A throughout the United States. Sally sells product B throughout the United States, and Ralph sells product C throughout the United States. Your company, of course, manufactures A, B, and C. All three salespeople know their individual product lines inside out and are experts in their fields. They each run up large expenses for air fares and hotels while traveling the country to sell their individual product lines. It may be worthwhile to continue this way. On the other hand, let's discuss a situation that could occur. Suppose your company is based in New York and Charlie is in San Francisco selling product A. One of Charlie's customers in San Francisco wants to talk about product B. Charlie has to say that he will have Sally call the customer since she is the specialist on product B. The customer asks, "Why can't you tell me? You're already here?" Charlie explains that the product is Sally's and she's the expert. If you're the sales manager, you can see that it may be beneficial to all your salespeople to sell products A, B, and C without having all of them traveling throughout the United States. You consider switching from product segmentation to territorial segmentation. You rearrange the U.S. sales territories roughly into three sections: Eastern, Central, and Western. Now, Charlie sells A, B, and C in the Eastern segment; Sally sells A, B, and C in the Central segment; and Ralph sells A, B, and C in the Western part of the United States.

Keep in mind that this is a major change! Your customers must get accustomed to dealing with new salespersons. Maybe Charlie had a long established friendship with a customer in California who bought your product because Charlie sold it. This doesn't happen you say? Sometimes it does. Maybe also Charlie enjoyed taking his family on some of his trips to the West Coast. Now, such trips will be more expensive and he must take them during his vacation because his work is confined to the East coast. From the customer's view, he may like discussing products A, B, and C with one salesperson. And the company's travel and sales expenses will decrease. The most important issue is to look at both segmentation methods and see which is best for your company, your customer, your product line, and your sales goals.

What Is a Sales Forecast?

The sales forecast is often not given the importance that it should have. The company budget should be based on a sales forecast. As an example, if you want to take a cruise or go on an expensive vacation next year, what do you usually do? You may say to yourself, "I'm earning $XX this year and I expect to be working here next year and get a raise of Y%, and therefore I think I can take this vacation." You make a decision by calculating a future major expense and taking into account your current and projected income. The same method is used in business.

The chief financial officer (CFO) of the company, in order to plan expenditures for next year, wants to know the anticipated income (represented by sales) for next year. The budget committee, in allocating funds to various departments for operations, wants to know the anticipated sales so that it can then plan the budget. Thus, both individuals and companies want to know what their probable income will be in order to plan their future expenditures. A sales forecast gives a company that information.

Generally, when you are ready to prepare your sales forecast, you will review a graph or other presentation of data showing sales over the past five to ten years. You will look at this trend and then take into consideration factors such as:

- Prevailing economic conditions
- New products that may boost sales
- Strategic sales and marketing planning including goals

- Your "gut feeling" about some customers that are ready to buy more than they currently buy

Forecasting is not as simple as some people think. They simply take the existing sales and multiply by 1.05. That is not the way to forecast. The process requires more thought than that. Your sales could increase or decrease markedly by such factors as what competition is entering or leaving the market, new technologies utilized by you or your competitors, new (or newly enforced) government regulations, and changing consumer preferences. You must take all these into account with your best estimates of their influences on the sales of your product and then make your estimate.

In addition to forecasting for budget purposes, managers in various areas of the company will want to be aware of the forecast because certain balance sheet items vary with anticipated sales. Items such as receivables, inventory, and accounts payable are subject to change based on varying sales. If sales are anticipated to increase significantly, then more inventories must be kept on hand, receivables will increase and so will expenses. Sales forecasting is worthy of a high level of respect. Many major company decisions may be based on it.

What Is the Function of a Sales Manager?

When a salesperson becomes a sales manager, his or her responsibilities change. Quite often, a person with the highest sales numbers is promoted to sales manager when an opening occurs. You may find some cases, however, in which salespeople on commission structures do not want to be sales managers. A salesperson may not want to be a sales manager and may not be good at it, but many companies consider their best salespersons as future sales managers. The toughest part of being promoted to sales manager *is to have to stop doing the old job*. This person may want to "keep a few of my old accounts." While allowing this may be appropriate in a few cases where customers buy from "Charlie" instead of the company, in most cases a new sales manager *should manage the sales department and let the sales staff sell*. The new responsibilities include reviewing territorial allocations, determining segmentation structure, hiring new salespersons, reporting to the vice president of sales, and similar responsibilities.

The same principle applies in scientific areas. Perhaps a really good chemist who produces many technical publications is promoted to department head on the basis of his skills and publications. If a bench chemist aspired to manage, becoming a department head would be his priority and he would learn management techniques and be people oriented, and probably make a good department manager. In cases where a promotion was based only on the highest number of publications, a real error may have been made. How do you prevent this? You set up a separate salary structure for the real producers and, if they have no interest in managing, provide them with some extra compensation for their extraordinary work. What applies to chemists also applies to salespeople. If you have a salesperson who is really good at selling and wants to continue, let him remain in the field to sell, pay him well, and don't burden him with other chores. The main point should be obvious. When you select a person to manage a department, make sure he has managerial abilities and is relieved from his previous job to concentrate on new responsibilities.

4
FINANCE

In the past, the finance area enjoyed its own "ivory tower"—much like research and development groups did and still do. Today, with increasing costs and increasing opportunities, all department managers should be aware of the principles necessary to run departments effectively and be able to provide accurate cost and expense information to financial managers of the company. This discipline is often called managerial finance. The topics that will be covered are:

- Management's primary goal
- Depreciation
- Debt and equity, interest and dividends
- Time value of money (most important concept in finance)
  - Present value
  - Future value
- Bond valuation
- Stock valuation
- Expected value
- Economies of scale and diminishing returns
- Financial statements
  - Profit and loss statement, income statement
  - Balance sheet
- Retained earnings
- Ratio analysis
- Capital budgeting
  - Payback period
  - Net Present Value
  - Internal rate of return
- Cash flow analysis
- Operating leverage
- Risk and rates of return

We now venture into the world of finance. *Many of the issues we will discuss will apply to decisions that you make every day in your life.* In business, these issues are simply on a larger monetary scale and apply to your company.

Management's Primary Goal

Management's primary goal is pure and simple: to maximize shareholder wealth by running the company so well that the common stock is in demand and its price increases. In the case of a sole proprietorship, the owner strives to make as much profit as possible. What's possible? If you keep raising the prices, your customers will find it beneficial to purchase from your competitor what they formerly bought from you. The market thus determines your maximum price within the conditions you set for your company: quality, price, delivery, and customer service. The price condition is subject to the principle of reverse effect covered in Chapter 2 on marketing. If you raise your price too high, customers will go elsewhere.

The shareholders (stockholders) of a corporation are the owners, and maximizing their share value is management's goal. As a manager, how will you know that the value of your company's stock has been maximized? Well, you won't, but you'll believe you came close. For example, if the stock during your first year as president rose from $20 to $30 per share and you think that that's great, stockholders may say that it should have gone to $32. The increase indicates you performed well and you may believe you "maximized" the value at $30. You know value and you know whether you achieved your goals, but you can never know whether you "maximized" the stock value.

Depreciation

You must know two facts about depreciation: it is a non-cash item and it is an expense. Therefore, it is a non-cash expense and is treated as a tax deduction. Because depreciation is a non-cash expense, financial managers and accountants look at it differently. An accountant lists depreciation in appropriate records such as an income statement and balance sheet. A financial manager is primarily interested in cash

Table 4.1 Classes and Asset Lives Assigned by 1986 Tax Reform Act

CLASS (YEARS)	PROPERTY
3	Computers and research equipment
5	Cars, other vehicles, some computers
7	Office furniture and fixtures, most industrial equipment
10	Some industrial equipment
27.5	Residential real property
31.5	Nonresidential real property, i.e., commercial and industrial buildings

flows on the premise that cash flows determine how well the business is performing.

The financial manager realizes that, as a tax deduction, depreciation reduces net operating income (earnings before interest and taxes [EBIT]), and thereby reduces the taxes to be paid. This, of course, is good, but it does not indicate how well the company is run, especially if most of the assets depreciated were purchased years ago (maybe when the company was run by someone else). The cash flows determine performance—how the company is running now.

Congress changes the permissible tax depreciation methods on occasion. Table 4.1 illustrates some permitted asset lives. Current information about the different classes of deductible items and the time periods over which the depreciation can be applied are best obtained by going to the Internal Revenue Service website www.IRS.gov and typing "depreciation" in the search box. Among the selections listed will be IRS Publication 946 (2007) titled *How to Depreciate Property*. This publication contains a wealth of information that will enable you to know which assets you can depreciate and over what time period. Here is an excerpt from the IRS website on December 8, 2008:

"A Brief Overview of Depreciation

Depreciation is an income tax deduction that allows a taxpayer to recover the cost or other basis of certain property. It is an annual allowance for the wear and tear, deterioration, or obsolescence of the property.

Most types of tangible property (except, land), such as buildings, machinery, vehicles, furniture, and equipment are depreciable. Likewise, certain intangible property, such as patents, copyrights, and computer software is depreciable.

In order for a taxpayer to be allowed a depreciation deduction for a property, the property must meet all the following requirements:

- The taxpayer must own the property. Taxpayers may also depreciate any capital improvements for property the taxpayer leases.
- A taxpayer must use the property in business or in an income-producing activity. If a taxpayer uses a property for business and for personal purposes, the taxpayer can only deduct depreciation based only on the business use of that property.
- The property must have a determinable useful life of more than one year.

Even if a taxpayer meets the preceding requirements for a property, a taxpayer cannot depreciate the following property:

- Property placed in service and disposed of in same year.
- Equipment used to build capital improvements. A taxpayer must add otherwise allowable depreciation on the equipment during the period of construction to the basis of the improvements.
- Certain term interests.

Depreciation begins when a taxpayer places property in service for use in a trade or business or for the production of income. The property ceases to be depreciable when the taxpayer has fully recovered the property's cost or other basis or when the taxpayer retires it from service, whichever happens first.

A taxpayer must identify several items to ensure the proper depreciation of a property, including:

- The depreciation method for the property
- The class life of the asset
- Whether the property is "Listed Property"
- Whether the taxpayer elects to expense any portion of the asset

- Whether the taxpayer qualifies for any "bonus" first year depreciation
- The depreciable basis of the property

The Modified Accelerated Cost Recovery System (MACRS) is the proper depreciation method for *most* property. Additional information about MACRS, and the other components of depreciation are in Publication 946, How to Depreciate Property.

A taxpayer must use Form 4562, Depreciation and Amortization, to report depreciation on a tax return. Form 4562 is divided into six sections and the Instructions for Form 4562 contain information on how, and when to fill out each section."

Now we return from the IRS statement to our discussion.

Remember, check with the Internal Revenue Service or your accountant (who should have checked with the IRS) to learn the current depreciation categories and allowances. If your business is large enough to have an accountant handle its financial records, he or she will understand depreciation and the different classes of property such as computers and research equipment, cars, buildings, industrial equipment, and their allowable depreciation schedules.

It is worth repeating the point that depreciation reduces net operating income and thereby reduces the company's taxes. That may be good, but it doesn't indicate how well a company is run. Sales and earnings are the factors that show you how well a company is run.

Debt and Equity

Two methods of financing an enterprise are debt and equity. A company can incur a debt by issuing bonds. A bond issue does not alter control of the business. The business makes periodic interest payments to the bondholders and ultimately pays back the original amount owed. Bondholders cannot tell you how to run the company. If a company is financed by equity, it sells stock, in essence "a piece of the action." The company may choose to pay dividends. Because the common stockholders are part owners of the business, they can tell you how to run the company.

Stocks and Bonds

Generally, the "stocks" term covers common stock issued by public companies. A private company may issue stock to a few persons, but most company stocks are issued by public corporations. In order for a company to "go public" and sell stock, it must meet requirements set by the U.S. Securities and Exchange Commission (SEC). After stock has been issued, the SEC continues to impose certain requirements. A public corporation must make its income and expenses known to the public because public money was exchanged for the shares of company stock. In a private company, financial information is disclosed only to the IRS and not the general population.

The value or worth of a company is always stated in terms of its common stock. This is good to keep in mind as you learn more about business finances. Preferred stock is a different class of equity. It is a "hybrid" in the sense that it is considered by some to be somewhere between a bond and a share of common stock. More about preferred stock later in this chapter.

When a company issues shares of common stock, it sells a "piece of the action." Persons who purchase do so for two reasons, both of which relate to their income. First, they want the company (and thus their stock) to increase in value, so their stock will be worth more to them to keep or sell at a profit. This increase is called a capital gain. The second income source is the dividend payout by the company to shareholders. A company is not required to pay dividends. After a company has computed its sales for the year (or other time period, such as a quarter) and subtracted its expenses such as costs of sales, interest, payments, taxes, etc., what remains is net income available to common shareholders. This income can be reinvested back into the business or paid as dividends to shareholders. Funds poured back into the business are called retained earnings, although the term is misleading. Retained earnings are not "retained" in a drawer or file cabinet. They are used to improve the business, i.e., hire more people or purchase new machinery.

Some companies have never paid dividends but have chosen to reinvest income in the business as retained earnings. In those cases, the shareholders are looking only for capital gains increases and will not receive dividends. However, a company that has provided dividends

for a number of years would be unwise to not pay dividends in a particular quarter or year in order to reinvest the money back into the
business. This is true even if the company has excellent investment
opportunities. The reason is very simple. On paper, the company
appears to make forward strides by not paying dividends and rein-
vesting all profits back into the business, but the shareholders' view is
different. If the company has paid quarterly dividends for the past 10
years, shareholders received 40 consecutive dividends. Suddenly, the
company chooses not to pay dividends but to reinvest the funds along
with its normal portion of retained earnings. A typical shareholder is
not involved in running the business. He is simply an investor. Will
this shareholder really believe that the company has great investment
opportunities or is he going to think that something is wrong and the
company needs the money for something else? This is why it is unwise
to not pay a dividend after having paid a long string of dividends. The
failure to pay dividends may affect the confidence of the shareholders;
they may start selling their stock, thus driving the price down and
affecting the perceived value of the firm. Clearly, despite an excellent
investment opportunity, a company that has routinely paid dividends
would be wise to continue paying them.

There is another way to pursue the excellent investment opportunity. A company can chose to reinvest all the income back into the
business and issue a dividend in the form of stock shares instead of
cash. In essence, the company "retained" the money and reinvested it
and also made the shareholders happy because they received a dividend. This is easier said than done and it would be unwise to try
this more than once because some shareholders might see this step
as a dilution of ownership and the perceived value of the firm may
decrease.

Company bonds are issued with the promise of paying interest
normally at a rate higher than the dividend rate. For example, a dividend, calculated over a year (whether paid annually or quarterly) can
be 6, 8, or 10%. The interest rate on a bond may be 15%. Why do
the rates differ? A primary factor here is that the interest paid on a
bond is a tax deduction for the company. Dividend payments are not
tax deductions; they are paid after taxes are paid to the government.
Therefore, when a company pays a bond interest rate of 15%, it would
have had to pay much of that money in taxes had it not issued the

bond and made the promise of payment. Therefore, the "effective" interest payment can be looked upon as below 15%. The other reason to pay a little more to bondholders is because they have no say in how you run the company. Bondholders are not owners; they are investors. Unlike shareholders, who have a say, bondholders have no control over the company.

Let's examine a typical bond, for example, a $1,000 bond with a term of 10 years and an annual interest rate of 15%. The purchaser of the bond buys it from your company through underwriters for $1,000. The company will pay the purchaser $150 (15% of $1,000) each year for the next 10 years. At the end of the tenth year, when the tenth payment of $150 is due, the company will also return the $1,000 back to the bondholder. Of course, bonds can be sold from investor to investor, usually through brokers in the market. Our example assumes one person held the bond for its entire term and would receive all the payments. The company is obligated to make the payments regardless of who holds the bond.

It seems that the company is paying $2,500 for $1,000, and on paper, that is the case: 10 years × $150 equals $1,500 plus the original $1,000. However, since the value of money decreases over time, the second year's $150 is not worth as much as the first year's $150, and the third year's $150 payment is worth even less, and so on through the tenth year. This decrease in value is covered in the discussion of discounted cash flow analysis later in this chapter. In the tenth year when the $1,000 is repaid, that $1,000 is not worth nearly that at current dollar value. In addition, the company's tax deduction (for the interest) further reduces the cost to the company.

One variation on the bond theme is the convertible bond—a bond that may be converted to stock or another asset at a subsequent time at some subsequent value. A convertible bond would specify the conditions, for example, "One bond can be converted into XX shares of YY stock at a price of $ZZ. This is good until [date]."

Preferred stock is a hybrid; it is a stock by definition. The difference is in the "preferred" description. Shareholders who hold these stocks are "preferred." Dividends are always paid first to holders of preferred stock. This is not required by law, but it is a tradition that encourages people to buy preferred stock. The other advantage is that preferred stock ranks higher than common stock as a security issue. If a company must liquidate its assets, the bondholders are paid first, after the sales of assets, followed by preferred shareholders; the common shareholders are last in line. In fact, if a company is in enough trouble to have to liquidate, it is likely that nothing will be left for the common shareholders.

Hopefully, now you see how bonds, preferred stock, and common stock differ from each other. How do they differ from an investor's view? This is a matter of personal preference. Does the investor want a guaranteed income (yield, interest payments) and the security of knowing what he will receive each year, or does he want the capital gains, probable dividend payments, and the ownership and voting rights of common shareholders? The investor's preference determines the type of investment.

What difference does the issuance of bonds or stocks make from the company's view? Is the company willing to have other people control the company such as would be the case if it issued common stock? Of course, the company does not have to pay dividends if it issues common stock because dividends are not promised, as interest payments on a bond are. A company can choose to issue bonds, promise to pay annual interest along with repaying the original value at the end of the term, and be certain that bondholders will have no say in management of the company.

Another factor comes into play after your first issue of stocks or bonds reaches the market. If you issued stock initially, and then need money for expansion a few years later, it may be advisable to use the debt mechanism of issuing bonds so you don't dilute the company value too much by issuing additional stock. On the other hand, if you already have a bond issue on the market, you may find it wise to issue stock instead. An additional bond issue would be considered more risky and would therefore need a higher yield. If you start issuing bonds behind another that's already in the market, the investment community knows you are already obligated to make payments to existing bondholders. In effect, investors will consider the second issue more risky and want higher interest payments in return for lending your company money.

Time Value of Money: The Single Most Important Concept in Finance

The concept of the time value of money simply means that you take money spent or received at a time in the past or at a time in the future and you equate that to its Present Value. Alternatively, you can take money spent or received in the past or spent or received now, and equate that to what it will be worth at some point in the future.

In the course of long range planning for a business, you will be considering an investment to be made today or maybe next year and you will look at the anticipated returns perhaps five years from now. When you anticipate a particular dollar value return, say, five years from now, you are interested in what that amount of money would be worth today or the day you make the investment. This permits a better evaluation of projects and investments.

Not all projects start producing cash inflows at the same time; however, when you equate them to today's dollars you have a basis for a comparison. This projection is called calculating Present Value. When you do the reverse operation and equate an amount to what it will equal at a particular point in the future you are determining Future Value. What happens when you equate a figure in the past? Well, there are two things to consider. First, there is nothing you can do about the past except learn from it. Second, if you equate a figure in the past, you will still refer to the starting date of an investment as Present Value and the ending period as Future Value. This involves the principle of compounding. Table 4.2 illustrates the compounding

Table 4.2 Compound Interest Calculations

YEAR	CALCULATION	INTEREST EARNED PV(k)
1	$100.00 × 1.07 = $107.00	$7.00
2	107.00 × 1.07 = 114.49	7.49
3	114.49 × 1.07 = 122.50	8.01
4	122.50 × 1.07 = 131.08	8.58
5	131.08 × 1.07 = 140.26	9.18
		$40.26

Formula: Amount at beginning of year, PV × (1 + k) = Amount at end of year, FV_n.

of $100 over a five-year period, and the details are given in the subsequent text.

When you evaluate investments, the Present Value is the starting value of the investment, whenever that occurred or will occur. The Future Value is the ending value whenever that occurred or will occur. For example, if you're planning to make an investment next year and the "term" over which you are going to evaluate it is five years, the Present Value is the value that the money will have next year (one year from now). The Future Value is the value of the investment six years from now (at the end of the five-year term). To reiterate, the Present Value is the starting value; the Future Value is the ending value, regardless of when the investment commenced. Calculating the value in the future is generally called *compounding*. When we calculate in the other direction, the operation is called *discounting*. Let's look at an example of compounding to clarify the principle.

Assume you want to deposit $100 in a bank and are told by the bank that the interest rate is 7%. First, you want to check to see whether the 7% is simple interest or compound interest. If you leave the $100 in the bank for five years at simple interest, you will get $7 each year for five years, or a total of $35 interest; your account would total $135. At the end of the first year at compound interest, your $100 would have gained $7, giving you $107; at the end of the second year, the $107 would gain 7% and you would earn $7.49 on that $107. During the third year, you have the $100 plus $7 plus $7.49 in your account and you will receive $8.01 interest on that, and so on, as illustrated in Table 4.2. At the end of five years, you will have gained $40.26 interest and now have $140.26 in your account.

You may say, "That is only $5.26 more than the $135 I would have had with simple interest." Well, your goal is to maximize profit so therefore, you should always seek a higher value. Note that when you compare $40.26 to $35.00, the $40.26 is 15% greater. Additionally, as interest rates or rates of return on investments increase beyond 7 to 14, 18, 25%, etc., these differences become greatly magnified. Another factor to consider is that your business involves far more than $100 and you may be investing millions of dollars. Based on millions of dollars and rates of return around 20 to 30%, the values are very significant. Take a look at this mathematically by setting it up in equation form:

PV = Present Value of your account (or beginning amount of $100)

k = bank interest rate, 7% per year, or 0.07 expressed as a decimal*

I = dollars of interest earned during the year = k(PV)

FV_n = Future Value or ending amount of account at the end of n years

n = number of years, or, more generally, periods involved in investment

To clarify, PV is the value now, at the *present* time; FV_n is the value n years into the future after compound interest is earned. Note also that FV_0 is the Future Value *zero* years into the future, which is the *present*, so $FV_0 = PV$.

In our example, n = 1, so $FV_n = FV_1$ calculated as follows:

$$FV_1 = PV + I$$
$$= PV + PV(k)$$
$$= PV(1 + k) \qquad\qquad (4\text{-}1)$$

In words, the *Future Value* (FV) at the end of one period is the *Present Value* multiplied by the quantity (1 plus the interest rate). We can now use Equation 4-1 to calculate how much your $100 will be worth at the end of one year at 7% interest:

$$FV_1 = \$100(1 + 0.07) = \$100(1.07) = \$107$$

Your account will earn $7 of interest (I = $7) and you will have $107 at the end of the year. Now, as we stretch the equation taking into account each of the five years in our example, we get the following:

$$FV_5 = PV(1 + k)(1 + k)(1 + k)(1 + k)(1 + k)$$
$$= PV + (1 + k)^5$$
$$= PV(1.07)^5$$
$$= PV(1.4026)$$

Instead of performing that somewhat lengthy calculation each time, we can set up a chart. We can calculate what we will call a Future

---

* On financial calculators the term i is frequently used rather than k.

Value Interest Factor (FVIF) for various combinations of time periods and percentages. To determine rate based on a combination of time period and percentage rate of return, we can simply refer to the chart and use that factor (see Table 4.3). Actually, many computer programs include these calculations and many small portable calculators are programmable to make these calculations. However, this chart is both convenient and clearly shows the progression in this type of calculation. Table 4.3 is set up for a value of $1. Therefore, when you set your Present Value, you simply multiply the number of dollars by the factor for $1 to get an answer.

Another significant concept here is the *period*. The reason for use of this term is that periods are not always years. For example, if our illustration of 7% over five years were presented with semiannual compounding, the result would be ten compounding periods and n would equal 10. Based on semiannual compounding and an annual interest rate of 7%, the actual interest rate or rate of return (k) would be 3.5%. Pay careful attention to how an interest rate or rate of return is quoted and adjust if necessary for the time period. Additionally, pay strict attention to the compounding and adapt accordingly.

Let's look at another example of this interest rate and time relationship. If you were considering a situation that would provide a return of 12% annually over a term of five years and the compounding was quarterly, the number of periods is 5 years × 4 quarterly compounds = 20. At the same time, since the interest rate was quoted as 12% annually, the quarterly interest rate will be 1/4 × 12 = 3%. So here you would have n = 20 and k = 3. It makes a big difference!

Discounting is the reverse of compounding or, in mathematical terms, it is the *inverse* of compounding. Discounting comes into play if you want to know how many dollars to invest today to receive a certain number of dollars in the future based on a specific rate of return. We know the Future Value (to be received), the rate of return, and the number of compounding periods and use them to calculate the Present Value (to be invested). We will rearrange Equation 4-1, which is FV = PV (1 + k). When solving for PV, we divide both sides by (1 + k):

$$PV = \frac{FV_n}{(1+k)^n} = FV_n(1+k)^{-n} = FV_n\left(\frac{1}{1+k}\right)^n$$

$$(4\text{-}2)$$

Table 4.3 Future Value of $1 at End of n Periods

PERIOD (n)	1%	2%	3%	4%	5%	6%	7%	8%	9%	10%
1	1.0100	1.0200	1.0300	1.0400	1.0500	1.0600	1.0700	1.0800	1.0900	1.1000
2	1.0201	1.0404	1.0609	1.0816	1.1025	1.1236	1.1449	1.1664	1.1881	1.2100
3	1.0303	1.0612	1.0927	1.1249	1.1576	1.1910	1.2250	1.2597	1.2950	1.3310
4	1.0406	1.0824	1.1255	1.1699	1.2155	1.2625	1.3108	1.3605	1.4116	1.4641
5	1.0510	1.1041	1.1593	1.2167	1.2763	1.3382	1.4026	1.4693	1.5386	1.6105
6	1.0615	1.1262	1.1941	1.2653	1.3401	1.4185	1.5007	1.5869	1.6771	1.7716
7	1.0721	1.1487	1.2299	1.3159	1.4071	1.5036	1.6058	1.7138	1.8280	1.9487
8	1.0829	1.1717	1.2668	1.3686	1.4775	1.5938	1.7182	1.8509	1.9926	2.1436
9	1.0937	1.1951	1.3048	1.4233	1.5513	1.6895	1.8385	1.9990	2.1719	2.3579
10	1.1046	1.2190	1.3439	1.4802	1.6289	1.7908	1.9672	2.1589	2.3674	2.5937

Formula: $FVIF_{k,n} = (1 + k)^n$

From Equation 4-2, you see how discounting, or going from Future Value back to Present Value, is the inverse of compounding. Here again we can make various calculations and set up a table. In fact, we have done so. Table 4.4 shows the Present Value Interest Factor (PVIF) for $1 over ten periods.

Using the same details as in our compounding example, we can ask, "If I can get a rate of return on investment of 7% compounded annually for five years and I want to earn $140.26, how much will I have to invest now to do that?"

$$PV = FV_5 \, (PVIF_{7\%, \, 5 \, Years})$$
$$= 140.26(0.7130)$$
$$= \$100$$

This example was based on our previous data and therefore worked out to precisely $100. In real life, your question may be, "If I want $100,000 in three years and I can have annual compounding with an annual interest rate of 10%, how much must I invest now?" Look at Table 4.4. Check the line for three compounding periods and the column for 10%. The figure is 0.7513. If you multiply 0.7513 by $100,000 (the amount you want in three years) you would have to invest $75,130 now at 10% compounded annually to have $100,000 in three years.

Another key point to remember when you have a problem such as this to work out is that you are always dealing with four variables: Present Value, Future Value, rate of return, and number of periods. When you know any three, you can always calculate the fourth. If you only know two you cannot calculate the other two. You need more information.

How do you calculate the interest rate? Well, if you know the Present Value and Future Value, you can divide the Present Value by the Future Value to obtain the PVIF. Now look at Table 4.4 to find the rates and find k. In fact, you can do this two ways. If you choose to divide the Present Value by the Future Value, you will get the PVIF and can look up k on the PVIF factor table. If you choose to divide the Future Value by the Present Value, you will get the Future Value interest factor (FVIF). If you know the number of periods, you can look up the rate (k) in the Future Value interest chart (Table 4.5).

Another important point will prevent you from making a common error. Remember, when you are talking about the future you always want your money to grow, so your FVIF is going to be greater than 1.

Table 4.4 Present Value of $1 Due at End of n Periods

PERIOD (n)	1%	2%	3%	4%	5%	6%	7%	8%	9%	10%
1	.9901	.9804	.9709	.9615	.9524	.9434	.9346	.9259	.9174	.9091
2	.9803	.9612	.9426	.9246	.9070	.8900	.8734	.8573	.8417	.8264
3	.9706	.9423	.9151	.8890	.8638	.8396	.8163	.7938	.7722	.7513
4	.9610	.9238	.8885	.8548	.8227	.7921	.7629	.7350	.7084	.6830
5	.9515	.9057	.8626	.8219	.7835	.7473	.7130	.6806	.6499	.6209
6	.9420	.8880	.8375	.7903	.7462	.7050	.6663	.6302	.5963	.5645
7	.9327	.8706	.8131	.7599	.7107	.6651	.6227	.5835	.5470	.5132
8	.9235	.8535	.7894	.7307	.6768	.6274	.5820	.5403	.5019	.4665
9	.9143	.8368	.7664	.7026	.6446	.5919	.5439	.5002	.4604	.4241
10	.9053	.8203	.7441	.6756	.6139	.5584	.5083	.4632	.4224	.3855

Formula: $\displaystyle PVIF_{k,n} = \frac{1}{(1+k)^n} = \left(\frac{1}{1+k}\right)^n$

Table 4.5 Future Value of Annuity of $1 per Period for n Periods

PERIOD (n)	1%	2%	3%	4%	5%	6%	7%	8%	9%	10%
1	1.0000	1.0000	1.0000	1.0000	1.0000	1.0000	1.0000	1.0000	1.0000	1.0000
2	2.0100	2.0200	2.0300	2.0400	2.0500	2.0600	2.0700	2.0800	2.0900	2.1000
3	3.0301	3.0604	3.0909	3.1216	3.1525	3.1836	3.2149	3.2464	3.2781	3.3100
4	4.0604	4.1216	4.1836	4.2465	4.3101	4.3746	4.4399	4.5061	4.5731	4.6410
5	5.1010	5.2040	5.3091	5.4163	5.5256	5.6371	5.7507	5.8666	5.9847	6.1051
6	6.1520	6.3081	6.4684	6.6330	6.8019	6.9753	7.1533	7.3359	7.5233	7.7156
7	7.2135	7.4343	7.6625	7.8983	8.1420	8.3938	8.6540	8.9228	9.2004	9.4872
8	8.2857	8.5830	8.8923	9.2142	9.5491	9.8975	10.2598	10.6366	11.0285	11.4359
9	9.3685	9.7546	10.1591	10.5828	11.0266	11.4913	11.9780	12.4876	13.0210	13.5795
10	10.4622	10.9497	11.4639	12.0061	12.5779	13.1808	13.8164	14.4866	15.1929	15.9374

Formula: $\displaystyle \text{FVIFA}_{k,n} = \sum_{t=1}^{n}(1+k)^{n-t} = \frac{(1+k)^{n}-1}{k}$

When you calculate Present Value, you are looking for an investment figure that is smaller than what you will have at the future date. That number, the PVIF, will be less than one. This may sound simple enough, but many people look in the wrong table and calculate in the wrong direction! Remember, when you calculate Future Value, the FVIF is greater than 1; when you calculate Present Value, the PVIF is less than 1.

Annuities

An annuity is an investment that involves a series of regular payments over a finite time period. There are two types: one in which the payment is made at the beginning of the time period and a second, in which the payment is made at the end of the time period. The latter is the most common and will be discussed here. The same principle applies to calculating either annuity type: you simply shift the time frame because the payments are made earlier in the first type. Here, however, we will consider the annuities involving payments made at the end of the time period. As with the individual lump sum payments discussed above, we have Present Value and Future Value. Table 4.5 shows Future Values of an annuity of $1 per period or n periods. Table 4.6 shows Present Value of an annuity of $1 per period or n periods. What we said about the Present Value factor being smaller than 1 does not hold because an annuity consists of a *series* of regular payments at regular intervals.

What if you have a series that is either not regular in time or not regular in amount invested? In that case, your investment is not an annuity. Several individual Present Value or Future Value problems will have to be solved individually and then combined.

This concept of discounted cash flow—a general term applied to the compounding and discounting processes—will come into play in many business calculations. As stated in the heading of this section, discounted cash flow is *the single most important concept in managerial finance,* and I hope that you see its application to some of the problems that you now face in your business. As you progress through this book, you will realize how important it is.

Table 4.6 Present Value of Annuity of $1 per Period for n Periods

PERIOD (n)	1%	2%	3%	4%	5%	6%	7%	8%	9%	10%
1	0.9901	0.9804	0.9709	0.9615	0.9524	0.9434	0.9346	0.9259	0.9174	0.9091
2	1.9704	1.9416	1.9135	1.8861	1.8594	1.8334	1.8080	1.7833	1.7591	1.7355
3	2.9410	2.8839	2.8286	2.7751	2.7232	2.6730	2.6243	2.5771	2.5313	2.4869
4	3.9020	3.8077	3.7171	3.6299	3.5460	3.4651	3.3872	3.3121	3.2397	3.1699
5	4.8534	4.7135	4.5797	4.4518	4.3295	4.2124	4.1002	3.9927	3.8897	3.7908
6	5.7955	5.6014	5.4172	5.2421	5.0757	4.9173	4.7665	4.6229	4.4859	4.3553
7	6.7282	6.4720	6.2303	6.0021	5.7864	5.5824	5.3893	5.2064	5.0330	4.8684
8	7.6517	7.3255	7.0197	6.7327	6.4632	6.2098	5.9713	5.7466	5.5348	5.3349
9	8.5660	8.1622	7.7861	7.4353	7.1078	6.8017	6.5152	6.2469	5.9952	5.7590
10	9.4713	8.9826	8.5302	8.1109	7.7217	7.3601	7.0236	6.7101	6.4177	6.1446

Formula: $\text{PVIFA}_{k,n} = \sum_{t=1}^{n} \dfrac{1}{(1+k)^t} = \dfrac{1 - \dfrac{1}{(1+k)^n}}{k} = \dfrac{1}{k} - \dfrac{1}{k(1+k)^n}$

Bond Valuation

We have already mentioned that the payment on a bond is comprised of a series of regular, usually annual, payments of interest, plus repayment of the original investment at the end of the term. If for example, you purchased a $1,000, 10-year, 15% annual interest bond and continued to hold it, you would have given the issuer $1,000 at the beginning. At the end of the first year and subsequent years, you would have received $150 from the issuer, until the end of the tenth year, at which time you would receive $150 for interest plus your $1,000 investment back.

The return represents two difference sources of funds. The $150 (in this case) you received at the end of each year for ten years. Therefore, you have a regular series of payments made at regular time intervals, and therefore you have an annuity. You also have the original $1,000 returned at the end of the 10 years, but it will not have the same value as $1,000 today. The method for valuing a bond is a discounted cash flow calculation that is really the sum of two different cash flow problems. Look now at the equation used to find a bond's value

$$\text{Value} = V = \text{the sum of } I\left(\frac{1}{1+k}\right)^t + M\left(\frac{1}{1+k}\right)^n$$

$$= I(\text{PVIFA}_{k,n}) + M(\text{PVIF}_{k,n})$$

where:

I = amount of interest paid each period
M = par value or maturity value ($1,000 in this case)
k = rate of interest on bond
n = number of payment periods until bond matures
t = time period of annuity

Typically, when an annuity and lump sum payment are discounted, the total will equal the original value of the bond. In this case, even though 10 × $150 interest = $1,500 + $1,000 investment = $2,500, when all this is discounted back to terms of today's dollars, the value will amount to $1,000. Note also that the calculation is simplified by using the Present Value Interest Factor for an annuity (PVIFA) from Table 4.6. The factor for discounting the lump sum payment is

PVIF from Table 4.4. Although the calculation requires two different mechanisms, it is not difficult.

In reality, bonds are sold by one holder through the market, to another holder. The way to determine the value of a bond is to use a suitable factor n for the number of years remaining on the bond. For example, if a ten-year term bond is sold from one bondholder to another after four years, the value of the bond is determined via the same equations but letting n equal the remaining six years when you consult the appropriate PVIFA and PVIF tables. This will allow you to determine a suitable value to use for the sale or purchase of a bond held for some time.

Stock Valuation

Common stocks are valued by looking at two sources of gain: dividend yield and the actual gain in value of a share of stock. If you purchase a share of stock you are usually hoping to receive a dividend and a gain in stock value as the company increases its value. In equation form, this is presented as:

$$\begin{matrix} \text{Expected Rate of} \\ \text{Return} \end{matrix} = \begin{matrix} \text{Expected} \\ \text{Dividend Yield} \end{matrix} + \begin{matrix} \text{Expected Growth} \\ \text{Rate or Capital} \\ \text{Gains Yield} \end{matrix}$$

$$k = \frac{D}{P} + g$$

where:
  D = amount of dividend per share
  P = price paid per share

Here, as with bonds, we have two mechanisms by which the value of the stock will increase. The difference between this and the bond equation is that the stock equation does not apply discounting because we are seeking a rate of return, not an absolute number. A bond is issued at a specified price and rate of return, and therefore discounted figures apply. A common stock is valued by computing a rate of return, more correctly called an *expected rate of return*, and therefore no value needs to be discounted. In the case of a stock, the rate of return is not known in advance, and therefore the stock price cannot be discounted.

The market price of a stock should parallel the growth and value of the issuing company. This generally occurs, although depending on the industry, a time lag may occur between the growth of value and its reflection through an increase in the market price of the stock. Also, some companies do not grow but pay a constant stream of dividends. For example, some utility companies serve relatively small communities, experience no growth, and pay dividends routinely. How do you value these stocks? Use the same equation but keep in mind that g = 0. The equation then reduces to calculating dividend rate.

Expected Value

Expected value is a term used in stock and bond valuation that really means the expected return. The same term is used in another context. This may seem confusing, but you will understand the difference based on the way the term is used. For example, when someone wants to find the expected value of a bond, the term associated with bond valuation should be used. If, however, you want to evaluate alternative investments based on the *expected value* of the returns, you will be using the term as described here. The expected value of a project equals the possible return from the project multiplied by the probability that it will occur. An example can best illustrate this.

Suppose you were considering projects A, B, and C and could select only one, i.e., they are mutually exclusive. You can choose whichever one you want. You know a particular amount associated with the return on each project and you know the probability that the return will occur. For example, project A has a 50% probability of returning $100,000. The other 50% represents a zero return; there is no other possibility. Project B has a 20% probability that it will return $120,000 to you; it will either return $120,000 or nothing. Project C has a 30% probability of returning $150,000 to you.

If you select these on the basis of the return, you will select Project C because it has the largest potential return of $150,000. However, there is only a 30% probability that it will occur. Keeping in mind that the probabilities must total 100%, we see that A and B total the other 70%. When you multiply the return by the probability of occurrence, for instance, multiplying for project A, 0.5 × $100,000 = "expected value" of $50,000. Multiplying the probability of occurrence by the

Table 4.7 Expected Value

PROJECT	PROBABILITY OF OCCURRENCE (%)	RETURN ($)	EXPECTED VALUE ($)
A	50	100,000	50,000
B	20	120,000	24,000
C	30	150,000	45,000

anticipated return (if, in fact, the project succeeded), the result is called the expected value.

Remember, you will never actually realize this exact number. It's only a mathematical expression representing a function of the probability of the return if it comes in. Project A will give you either $100,000 or zero. It will not give you $50,000; the $50,000 represents the term called expected value. After you calculate the expected value for each project, you have a basis for comparison.

Some people use this method to decide which project to pursue. There are many other people who don't care to use this method at all. It is not presented here as a recommended procedure (see Table 4.7). It is described so that you will know that it is an alternative method by which you can view relationships among various projects. In actuality, expected value is a misleading term because you will not attain it. It's another tool in your management toolbox that you can use or not.

Economies of Scale

This term indicates that as a quantity or production of an item increases, its incremental cost decreases. As an example, assume you are ordering letterhead paper from a printer. The printer quotes a price of $125 for 1,000 sheets. When you ask how much for 2,000 sheets, the printer says $160 and you quickly calculate that it will cost you only $35 for the second 1,000 sheets. This continues on with larger quantities as indicated in Table 4.8. As quantities increase, the cost per thousand (incremental cost per thousand) decreases. The right column of the table shows the average cost that will also decrease with larger quantities if the incremental cost decreases.

What factors contribute to this result? The high cost of the first thousand sheets includes the printer's cost for setting up the printing

Table 4.8 Economies of Scale: Printing Letterhead

NUMBER OF COPIES	TOTAL COST ($)	INCREMENTAL COST PER 1,000 ($)	AVERAGE COST PER 1,000 ($)
1,000	125.00	125.00	125.00
2,000	160.00	35.00	80.00
5,000	250.00	30.00	50.00
10,000	375.00	25.00	37.50

press for your job. That's a fixed cost that will not be repeated with any increase in number of copies. The printer also had to mix the proper inks to get the color you wanted and order a minimum quantity of paper in the color and texture you selected. He may have 9,000 sheets left from the minimum quantity after he printed your 1,000 sheets that he may be able to sell to someone else. After all these components are handled, the printer incurs costs for the running of the press.

Economies of scale occur when a salesperson has to fly to a distant town to visit a client. Since the airfare will be incurred regardless of how many clients are visited, it seems worthwhile to try to schedule other clients or potential new ones during that visit. In the same manner as the incremental cost for letterhead was brought down, the incremental cost per visit to clients or potential clients may be reduced.

Diminishing Returns

This region of diminishing returns is analogous to a reversal of economies of scale. That is, there is a point beyond which you have to incur extra cost which means expending some additional effort in order to keep the system in line. Let's say that in the case of the printing press and the letterhead, that because of the nature of the press, it has to be reregistered, or shut down and re-adjusted after every 10,000 copies. If this is not done, then the letters on the letterhead are not printed exactly where they should be and the result is inferior quality. Assuming that is the case with this particular press, if a customer orders 20,000 copies, after the first 10,000 copies the press must be re-adjusted, which is an additional cost in time and money. If this is not done, then inferior quality sheets are produced and, either the customer accepts the product, or more likely, the printer absorbs the cost of the rejected material. This is an example of diminishing returns. Although economies of scale were in effect up to the point of 10,000 copies, continuing beyond that without any adjustment resulted in diminishing returns as exhibited by an inferior product.

Another example of this is when you are reading or studying. During your first hour, you may absorb much material. During your second hour, you may absorb almost as much. You will find during the fifth or sixth hour that you are not learning any more than you would in five or ten minutes of the first hour. You are now in the area of diminishing returns and it's best to get some rest and then start over.

Understanding Financial Statements

The key financial statements are the income statement and balance sheet. The income statement lists sales, costs, and expenses involved in obtaining sales, interest paid for loans or bonds, and taxes paid. They are presented in a specific format, as illustrated in Table 4.9. The essence of any income statement is subtracting the costs and expenses associated with sales from the total sales figure. The remaining amount is called net operating income or earnings before interest and taxes (EBIT). It represents net earnings before you subtract interest payments and taxes. The next step is to subtract interest expenses from EBIT to find earnings before taxes, then subtract taxes from earnings before taxes to determine real net earnings, also called net income— what your company made as real profit during the period covered by the income statement. Net income is what you want to maximize.

An income statement covers a definite period, usually a year, but it can cover a quarter of a year or a month or whatever you want it to cover. The period covered must be specified in the title of the income statement as for the Falcon Company example in Table 4.9. It is important to know what period is represented by the statement.

When you work with numbers for larger corporations, the figures will usually be presented in thousands of dollars and that also should be mentioned in the heading of the income statement. This means a figure of $1,000 on the statement really represents $1,000 × 1,000 or $1,000,000. The very large companies will use millions of dollars as their units. This means, for example, that $300 on an income statement means $300,000,000.

Table 4.9 Falcon Company Income Statement (in Thousands of Dollars) for Year Ending December 31, 2009

Sales	3,200
Costs and Expenses	
Labor and Materials	2,200
Depreciation	100
Selling	25
General and Administrative	40
Mortgage	50
Total of Costs and Expenses Listed above	2,415
Net Operating Income or Earnings before Interest and Taxes (EBIT)	785
Less Interest Expense:	
Interest on Mortgage	35
Earnings before Taxes	750
Federal and State Taxes (at 40%)	300
Net Income	450

Note: The "Federal and State Taxes (at 40%)" figure is for illustration only. Percentages of state taxes vary and many firms pay less than the 40% cited here.

The income statement is also known as a profit and loss (P and L) statement and may also be called a profit and loss sheet, or a P and L report. Most income statements will be larger than the one presented in Table 4.9 because they will include stock and bond statistics and other information. If you understand Table 4.9, you will be able to understand more complex statements.

The balance sheet (Table 4.10) is another major statement. The balance sheet covers three categories of information: assets of the company, liabilities of the company, and equity or net worth (the difference between assets and liabilities). In fact, accountants use the following balance sheet equation:

$$\text{Assets} = \text{Liabilities} + \text{Equity}$$

However, many financial managers, marketing directors, and research and development directors prefer the equation to be written:

Table 4.10 Falcon Company Balance Sheet (in Thousands of Dollars), December 31, 2009

ASSETS		LIABILITIES AND EQUITY	
Cash	50	Accounts Payable	50
Accounts Receivable	300	Accrued Wages	12
Inventories	250	Accrued Taxes	70
Total Current Assets	600	Total Current Liabilities	132
Plant and Equipment	1,600	Mortgage	900
Less Depreciation	400	Total Long Term Debt	900
Net Plant and Equipment	1,200	Total Liabilities	1,032
Total Assets	1,800	Equity	768
		Total Liabilities and Equity	1,800

$$\text{Assets} - \text{Liabilities} = \text{Equity}$$

Remember, shifting something from one side of an equation to the other side simply changes the sign (plus or minus) of the shifted item. Thus, when we moved liabilities from the right side to the left, we put a minus in front of it. This makes very good sense. Sometimes the equation is simply written as:

$$A - L = E$$

The same thing applies on a personal basis. You have a house and car that may not be completely paid for. You have a boat that is completely paid for. To determine your net worth, add the market values of the assets like the house, car, and boat, and from the total subtract the amounts you owe on the mortgage on the house and the remaining payments on the car. The remainder is your net worth. Subtracting your debts from your assets indicates what you really have. A balance sheet fills the same function for a company.

One of the big differences between an income statement and a balance sheet is that an income statement covers a definite period during which the income was obtained. A balance sheet is, in essence, a photograph of your company at a moment in time. The date in the heading of the balance sheet will indicate the date of the "photograph." Some points about a balance sheet worth remembering are:

Assets are shown on the left side and liabilities are shown on the right side (usually). Assets are listed in order of their liquidity (ease with which they can be converted to cash). Of course, cash is the most liquid asset and is listed first. Plant and equipment are extremely valuable but they are not very liquid and usually appear near the bottom of the asset list.

Liabilities are listed in the order in which they will be paid in the event of a company liquidation. In companies owned by stockholders (not in our example), their equity, which represents ownership, is listed as a liability and appears near the bottom of the list. A company that must liquidate will probably not have enough assets to pay stockholders in any event.

An important point: the balance sheet *will always balance mathematically!* That doesn't mean you will always like the way it balances. For example, if you have $3,000,000 in assets and $4,000,000 in liabilities, your equity or net worth is –$1,000,000—not good even though the equation balances. If you have assets of $3,000,000 and liabilities of $1,000,000, you have an equity or net worth of $2,000,000. The equation balances and the equity is positive. You want the balance sheet to show a good equity figure. Shareholders' (stockholders') equity on the balance sheet is listed as a liability because it is a liability of the company to its shareholders.

Net income shown on an income statement may be "retained" as retained earnings (in reality, reinvested into the company), distributed as dividends to shareholders, or it can be split between retained earnings and dividends; the split is the usual case. Retained earnings are not kept; they are reinvested in expansion or other activities. The dividends, of course, represent a return shareholders usually expect and they come from the net income.

The distribution of dividends from net income results in double taxation: shareholders are taxed twice. Since a shareholder owns part of the company and the company paid taxes before dividends were distributed, the shareholder paid a portion of those taxes. After the taxes are paid and net income is calculated, a portion of net income is received by the shareholder as a dividend. The shareholder must note the dividend as income on his personal tax return and again pay a tax on it. In reality, you are taxed two and three times on many things in life. When you go to the theater, you pay for your tickets with income that has already been taxed and you pay an amusement tax to the city on that. When you buy gasoline for your car with your income that is net income, you pay a gasoline tax. And so on and so on with many other things you purchase. However, the principle of double taxation in the world of finance refers to taxes on dividends received by shareholders.

Ratio Analysis

Ratios tell more than absolute figures. The five categories of ratios are:

- Liquidity
- Asset Management
- Debt Management
- Profitability
- Market Value

Let's now look at *liquidity ratios*. The first of these is the current ratio:

$$\text{Current Ratio} = \frac{\text{Current Assets}}{\text{Current Liabilities}}$$

See how it got its name? It deals with current finances. Using our example of the Falcon Company and referring to the balance sheet (Table 4.10), we see that the current ratio is:

$$\frac{600}{132} = 4.5$$

Is that good or not good? You must compare your company to other companies in the same industry. You cannot compare an airline to a string of movie theaters or a bank. Where do you get the figures? These ratios are available in publications from companies like Standard and Poor's, Moody's, and Robert Morris Associates. However, if you don't want to pay for subscriptions, you can ask a reference librarian in a library near you to find them. Another accurate method is to obtain annual reports of your competitors, review the financial data sections, and calculate the ratios from the data you see there. Another usually free source of ratios is the professional or trade association of your field. Such associations are valuable sources of information. Your company pays an annual membership fee and is entitled to ask for (usually) free and significant information.

A quick or acid test ratio is:

$$\frac{\text{Current Assets} - \text{Inventories}}{\text{Current Liabilities}}$$

This equation says: do not count your inventory as a current asset. Subtract your inventories from your current assets as listed on the balance sheet and divide the result by your current liabilities. An interesting note here is that if you have any inventory, the ratio will be smaller than the one we just discussed because you are subtracting from the numerator. Therefore, the numerator is smaller, but you have the same denominator (current liabilities) and your ratio will be smaller. Always compare ratios only in your own industry.

Think for a minute about the difference between these two ratios. Carrying a very large (maybe even undesirably large) inventory could make your current ratio look good. However, subtraction of that inventory and subsequent calculation of the quick or acid test ratio will reveal more accurately the health of your company. The former is good to know and the latter provides additional information.

The next major category of ratios is *asset management.* It indicates how well you manage your assets. The first ratio is inventory turnover (sales divided by inventory). If you divide your annual sales by the average inventory on hand, the ratio will equal the number of times your inventory "turned over" during the course of the year.

$$\text{Inventory turnover} = \frac{\text{Annual sales}}{\text{Average inventory}}$$

Generally speaking, the smaller your profit margin, the larger the number of turnover times you'll need. For example, a large supermarket works on a small profit margin of 1 to 3%. However, the store turns its stock over several times every month (an average figure is used because each item has a different ratio). On the other hand, a jewelry store that shows a profit of at least 100% on every item may not turn over its stock even once in a year. The jewelry store can "tolerate" a low turnover ratio because the profit margin is so great on individual sales.

The next asset management ratio is total assets turnover (sales divided by total assets). Dividing annual sales by total assets will result in a ratio you can compare to others in your industry in order to check your performance.

$$\text{Total assets turnover} = \frac{\text{Annual sales}}{\text{Total assets}}$$

The key *debt management ratio* is debt to total assets and it is a good indication of the percentage of debt that your company "is carrying" (has incurred). Although a ratio is a pure number and is not expressed in units, it is usually expressed as a percentage. For example, if your debt is $5,000,000 and your total assets are $10,000,000 your debt ratio is 0.50, usually called a 50% debt ratio.

Profitability ratios are appropriately named. The various ratios measure profitability. Each of them relates the net income available to common stockholders to something else and, in each case, a ratio is obtained. Remember, the income statement (profit and loss sheet) showed the net operating income (earnings before interest and taxes or EBIT). Interest expense was subtracted from it to determine earnings before taxes, then taxes were subtracted to find net income. For a corporation that issued common stock and thus has common stockholders, net income is available to common stockholders, although many companies divide the income, giving some to common stockholders as dividends, and "retaining" some to reinvest in the business. The entire sum before division into those parts is called net income available to common shareholders or stockholders.

The next ratio is called profit margin on sales. Clearly, the profit margin on sales is a good indication of profitability and the calculation is self explanatory:

$$\frac{\text{Net Income Available to Common Stockholders}}{\text{Sales}}$$

The next profitability ratio is return on total assets (ROA). Again, the equation is self-explanatory and answers, "How much money did we make in relation to the assets we had to use?"

$$\frac{\text{Net Income Available to Common Stockholders}}{\text{Total Assets}}$$

The last profitability ratio is the return on common equity (ROE). This is:

$$\frac{\text{Net Income Available to Common Stockholders}}{\text{Common Equity}}$$

Subtract current liabilities from the total assets shown on the balance sheets. The liabilities include bonds and the value of your preferred stock. The equation yields total common equity consisting of retained earnings plus the value of the common stock.

The last ratio category is *market value*. The most important ratio in this group is the price-to-earnings ratio or the price per share of common stock divided by earnings per share of common stock. The price per share of common stock is what is paid for a share in the market. The earnings-per-share (EPS) value is the net income of the firm divided by the number of shares of common stock outstanding. The price-to-earnings ratio is used in the stock market for considering the value of the stock.

The five general categories of ratios described above, when used in comparison with companies in your own industry, will give you a good picture of the status of your company. Other categories can be created for your specific needs by using one value in relation to another to determine the health of your company. If you devise a new ratio and are not sure that it is common for your industry, use it to compute the ratios for competitors. How do you do that? Get copies of their annual reports, extract the numbers you need, and compute them. Obtaining copies of your competitors' annual reports is a very smart move. It allows you to compare your company with the competition and assess your performance.

Capital Budgeting

Capital budgeting involves the budgeting for and the computation of returns from capital projects. What's a capital project? It's a project that involves expenditures for capital items. What's a capital item? It can be a large $500,000 machine for your production facility, the addition of several new vehicles to your sales department's fleet, a major project for your research and development department, or construction of a new building.

You select the projects that are the most necessary which, in turn, will yield the most return on your investment. Suppose you planned two projects, A and B, and they were *mutually exclusive,* that is, you could not select both of them. You may select one and cannot carry out the other. This occurs in life every day. Perhaps you want to go to a ball game and the theater but the events are scheduled at the same time ten miles apart. You have to pick one or the other because they are mutually exclusive projects. Three common methods are used to determine return on projects. You use the one you prefer. Then you can determine which project will provide the greatest return, and select it. The three methods are:

- Payback Period
- Net Present Value (NPV)
- Internal Rate of Return (IRR)

The Payback Period method calculates the time (in years) required to repay the original investment. We can use the illustration in Table 4.11. Assume an expenditure of $5,000. (It could easily be $5,000,000 for a larger company, but we use small figures for simplicity.) For year 0, we have an outward cash flow of $5,000 (indicated by parentheses). The right column shows a cumulative cash flow of –$5,000, since no money has come in yet. At the end of year 1, $2,000 has flowed into the company so the $2,000 is listed in the cash flow column for year 1 and the cumulative cash flow becomes –$3,000; we initially spent

Table 4.11 Payback Period

YEAR	CASH FLOW	CUMULATIVE CASH FLOW
0	(5,000)	(5,000)
1	2,000	(3,000)
2	2,000	(1,000)
3	3,000	2,000
4	3,000	5,000
5	4,000	9,000

$5,000 and generated $2,000; the cumulative difference or net cash flow is −$3,000. We proceed in a similar fashion for years 2 and 3. In year 3, we have gone beyond the point at which our cash flows inward equal initial cash flow outward. Assuming that the cash flows were received linearly over the course of the year, we "paid back" our investment one-third of the way through year 3; thus our payback period was 2 1/3 years.

Some interesting aspects of the payback period calculation are:

- It assumes that the outward cash flow was spent all at once.
- It assumes that the cash flows inward occur linearly through-out the year.
- It is quick and easy to calculate and can be used to compare projects.
- Disadvantage: it does not consider the time value of money (discounted cash flow analysis).
- Disadvantage: it does not consider cash flows beyond the pay-back period.

In some cases, later cash flows inward can be very large, and a project not undertaken because it did not show rapid payback, may, *in the long run,* be the better one. If the initial cash flow outward is not a single large instantaneous payment, but rather a series of cash flows over time, simply treat them as negative items as they occur. If you are evaluating two or more projects on the basis of the payback period method, you would consider the one showing the earliest repayment as the "best," and so forth for the second and third place projects. Keep in mind that this calculation only considers the time required to pay back the initial investment; it does not consider overall total profit of the project.

In the *Net Present Value* (*NPV*) method, the net present values of cash flows are computed for each year of a project's anticipated or effective existence. A value is obtained for each project under consideration. The one with the greatest net present value is chosen first. The one with the next largest net present value is selected second and so on (see Table 4.12).

As an example of a net present value computation, let's use the same project analyzed in the payback period example. Table 4.11 shows cash flows in the second column and the cumulative cash flow

Table 4.12 Net Present Value (NPV) at 10% Cost of Capital

NPV =	$-5{,}000 + PV(2{,}000)_{1yr} + PV(2{,}000)_{2yr} + PV(3{,}000)_{3yr} + PV(3{,}000)_{4yr} + PV(4{,}000)_{5yr}$
NPV =	$-5{,}000 + 2{,}000(0.9091) + 2{,}000(0.8264) + 3{,}000(0.7513) + 3{,}000(0.6830) + 4{,}000(0.6209)$
NPV =	$-5{,}000 + 1{,}818.20 + 1{,}652.80 + 2{,}253.90 + 2{,}049.00 + 2{,}483.60 = 5{,}257.50$

in the right column with figures in parentheses indicating negative values. Assume the anticipated life of the project is five years.

In year 0 (today), a $5,000 expenditure or cash flow outward occurred. Subsequently, $2,000 was received as a positive cash flow in year 1, $2,000 in year 2, $3,000 in year 3, $3,000 in year 4, and $4,000 in year 5. Although the example indicates cash received, we are calculating at a point before the project begins. Thus we are calculating *anticipated* cash flows (not true received cash) to determine whether we will or will not implement the project. Be aware that all these calculations are made before the fact and all the numbers represent anticipated cash.

We will establish the cost of capital, that is, the interest at 10% to be paid on money borrowed for this project. In reality, figures are seldom even; we select easy numbers for this illustration so that you are not distracted from the main point of understanding these techniques. NPV is equal to the −$5,000 represented as the initial cash outflow. Using Table 4.4, $2,000 is calculated to its present value at the end of year 1. The other figures are computed in the same fashion and the entire equation is summed algebraically. This is shown in Table 4.12 as the original −$5,000 plus $2,000 times the PVIF (0.9091) for one year at 10%, plus $2,000 times 0.8264, the PVIF for two years at 10% and so on. The actual values have been computed and a positive value of $5,257.50 is obtained. Note that the parentheses used in Table 4.12 are mathematical notations of quantities, not the negative notations used in Table 4.11. In Table 4.12, the minus signs indicate negative numbers. We found the PVIFs in Table 4.4 and used them in the above calculation.

Is the result a good number or not a good number? The problem must be looked at in two ways. Absolutely speaking, you must determine whether you feel the number is a suitable return. Then, relatively speaking, you will compare the return to the other values obtained for the other projects under consideration and rate them according to the greatest return. That's how the net present value method works.

At this point, you may ask, "How do I know what the return will be four or five years from now?" Well, you don't really know. You can call what you are doing making a calculated guess, computing, or evaluating; you are performing a financial evaluation of a project. However, you will have research and development information, marketing and sales forecasts, marketing research information, and information from other areas of the company to use in your estimates of the return on investment. Along with your computations, you will have information from other sources to aid you in deciding what is or is not a suitable return.

The third method is *Internal Rate of Return (IRR)* and represents a variation of the net present value method. The internal rate of return, k, is the rate that, when placed in the net present value equation, will make the net present value equal zero. In the case of the five-year project and anticipated cash flows determined from the payback period method that we have been discussing, we set the NPV equation as shown in Table 4.13. Instead of using the 10% cost of capital, we set the NPV equal to zero and the rate that yields a zero result is calculated.

How do you solve for k? One way is by arbitrarily selecting a value (the selection won't really be arbitrary; you will have a feel for a good value to try) and using it in the NPV equation to see whether the NPV equals zero or not. If the NPV is positive, select a larger value of k, i.e., a greater rate of return, and try again. If the value obtained is negative, then k is too large and you must try again with a smaller value. After a couple of tries, you find the proper value.

You don't have to work out the equation as illustrated in Table 4.13. You can select a particular k, and look up the PVIF on Table 4.4 as we did when calculating NPV above, and solve the equation that way. Alternatively, a computer program can make the calculation in seconds.

Remember that the IRR method utilizes the same equation used for NPV, but it has been rearranged. Instead of using cost of capital and solving for NPV, you set the NPV to zero and solve for k—now called the rate of return. The evaluation of alternative projects becomes easier because these techniques will allow you to select those with the greatest rates of return.

Table 4.13 Internal Rate of Return (IRR)

$$NPV = \frac{-5,000}{(1+k)^0} + \frac{2,000}{(1+k)^1} + \frac{2,000}{(1+k)^2}$$

$$+ \frac{3,000}{(1+k)^3} + \frac{3,000}{(1+k)^4} + \frac{4,000}{(1+k)^5}$$

$$= 0$$

Solve for k.

Should you use the internal rate of return or the net present value since they're essentially the same mathematical equation? That is, pure and simple, your choice of what you feel comfortable using. Your selection of the payback period method, the net present value, or the internal rate of return really depends on what you think is best for the evaluation of choices and that is the one you will feel comfortable using.

The latter two methods take into account the time value of money whereas the payback period does not, but the payback period is a quick and easy comparison method. Remember also that during the anticipated life of a project, the total expenditures or cash outflows will not always occur early. They will usually be in smaller amounts during year 1 or 2 or further down the line, and may occur in the same time periods as incoming cash flows. Simply indicate the expenditures in the equations of whatever procedure you select and proceed with the calculations. Track cash outflows and dates and cash inflows and dates and enter the data accordingly for the method you choose.

Another method used successfully by some executives is "gut feeling." Many people who follow gut feeling are correct as often as those with less experience who use mathematical procedures. Those who successfully use gut feeling to make decisions acquired that wisdom of prediction through years of experience. A hunch or gut feeling used for business, sports, or other pursuit is actually a logical derivation determined so rapidly that the person is not aware of the steps in the decision making process. This method works some of the time; if it doesn't work consistently, the board of directors and stockholders will question the wisdom of decisions based on it. You can certainly use one method, for example, payback, for a particular type of project, and another such as NPV for another type of project. As long as you use the same method for projects in the same general category, you won't be labeled inconsistent.

Cash Flow

Financial managers are more concerned with cash flows than are accountants. A cash flow system represents the life blood of a business. What's the difference between cash flows examined by a financial manager and those in the accountant's ledger? Sales may be on credit; a credit sale registered in the accountant's books will not represent immediate cash flow in the financial manager's view. Taxes listed on the accountant's books for this year may not actually have to be paid until next year. The financial manager tracks cash flow from the date paid. Another big item is depreciation. Recall that depreciation is a *non-cash flow expense*. It is a deduction on an income statement but it does not represent cash flowing into or out of the business. Depreciation is the major factor that illustrates a difference between accounting net profit and a financial manager's cash flow analysis.

The operating cash flows can be larger or smaller than accounting profits during any given period, depending on the magnitude of taxes, depreciation, and credit sales and their timing. Financial managers study specific cash flow statements. This gives them a feel for how cash actually "flows" through a business in both directions.

Degree of Operating Leverage

The degree of operating leverage is the relationship of the change in earnings before interest and taxes (EBIT) with regard to a corresponding change in sales:

$$\text{Degree of Operating Leverage (DOL)} = \frac{\% \text{ change in EBIT}}{\% \text{ change in Sales}}$$

To illustrate this, assume your sales have increased from $200,000 to $250,000 and your EBIT has, during the same interval, increased from \$60,000 to \$80,000. The degree of operating leverage is calculated as follows:

$$DOL = \frac{\dfrac{80{,}000 - 60{,}000}{60{,}000}}{\dfrac{250{,}000 - 200{,}000}{200{,}000}} = \frac{33\%}{25\%} = 1.32$$

An examination of the equation shows that the higher the degree of operating leverage, the more the profits will change relative to a change in sales volume. This degree of volatility may occur upward or downward.

"Leverage" is also used to describe another aspect of financial management. A highly leveraged firm has borrowed a lot of money to operate. If you have a business and have no debts, your business is not leveraged. This is very beneficial. A "leveraged buyout" (LBO) is simply an arrangement by which a person or group of persons borrows a lot of money to buy a company. Generally speaking, the more leveraged the firm is, the more money it has borrowed to operate. We calculated a degree of operating leverage above as a useful management statistic and explained leverage as a method of buying a company. Don't confuse the two uses of the term.

Risks and Rates of Return

Much has been said and written about risks and rates of return. Risks can be visualized by the width of the band defined by the standard deviation in a Gaussian distribution pattern (see Chapter 6 on statistics). However, at this point, it is appropriate to discuss briefly the relationship of risks and rates of return.

Generally, the greater your risk, the greater the possibility of loss and/or the greater the value if you attain a positive return. In business, as in life, if you are conservative, you play safe and achieve small gains or incur small losses. Conversely, if you are a risk taker, your decisions can produce significant gains or large losses. Which philosophy is best? That question has no right or wrong answer because your comfort with risk taking is a function of your personality. If your personality matches the personality of a company (discussed in Chapter 1), for example, you're conservative and work for a conservative company, your relationship with the company will be successful. Know to what degree you take risks, find a company whose philosophy matches yours, and enjoy what you do.

5

BREAK-EVEN ANALYSIS

In this chapter we are going to explore break-even analysis and look at the following aspects:

- Definition
- Fixed and variable costs
- Assumptions
- Example of technique
- Nonlinear break-even analysis

The break-even point is the point at which the business neither makes a profit nor incurs a loss. It is the point at which the total of fixed and variable costs is exactly offset by the revenues. Of course, you want to make a profit, so the goal is always to generate revenue beyond the break-even point. For example, many kids set up lemonade stands. Assume their parents bought the wood for the stand, built the stand, and bought the sign, pitchers, glasses, and lemonade mix. The little entrepreneurs sell five glasses at 25¢ and are happy with their profit of $1.25. However, their parents know they spent $20 to set up the business and their initial costs have not been recovered.

They realize that 80 glasses must be sold to recover the investment and no profit will be made until the 81st is glass sold, and even then the entire 25¢ received per glass is not profit. In fact, the business must sell more than 80 glasses to approach profit because the 80 glasses covered only initial fixed costs. Revenues from the initial sales contribute in part to recovery of the fixed costs and in part to the variable costs associated with each glass of lemonade.

Break even analysis is that calculation which shows how many units of our product must be sold to cover the initial fixed costs and the variable costs associated with each of those items up to that point. Beyond that point, which is where we want to be, each unit sold has a part of the revenue recovering the variable costs associated with it and the other part is profit. This is so because the fixed costs have been recovered at the break even point, and now we are beyond that point, into the realm of PROFIT.

Fixed and Variable Costs

It is appropriate to categorize fixed and variable costs so that the difference is clearly understood. Some examples of fixed costs are:

- Executive and office salaries
- General office expenses
- Insurance
- Property taxes
- Interest
- Depreciation of plant and equipment

Some examples of variable costs include:

- Costs of goods sold
- Factory labor
- Sales commissions
- Raw materials used
- Direct labor
- Sales expenses

The key points are:

- Fixed costs are those which you incur regardless of whether or not you produce and/or sell any item. Take a look at the list. The items on it (and some others you may think of for your own business or department or division) are things on which you're spending money regardless of whether you do or do not produce a product. This cost is a single number that is associated with your company and/or your product line. It is not expressed as "per unit" because it is not related to the number of units.
- Variable costs relate directly to the number of units, and therefore are expressed as "per unit." Take a look at "raw materials used," the most recognizable variable cost. Obviously, the more items produced, the more raw materials used that must be replaced. This is why variable costs are expressed per

unit. In this discussion, a variable cost is constant per unit. Presenting this concept one more way, when the variable cost is constant per item and the total cost varies with the number of items produced, the variability is with the change of total cost based on the number of items produced.

- The fundamental break-even analysis is based on an assumption that all manufactured product is sold, i.e., no inventory remains unsold.
- Another assumption is no price breaks. While a company sets a certain price for which it sells product on a single unit basis, it will allow a price break or discount for large quantity purchases. This occurs in reality but is not included in our discussion here.
- We also assume that variable costs are constant (despite the seeming contradiction in terms). This does not occur in reality because overtime pay, factory labor and bonuses for exceeding production, and other expenditures will change the variable costs. Again, for purposes of simplicity, we assume that variable costs remain constant per unit.

Assumptions

The assumptions made above are not strong deterrents to obtaining accurate figures and we will illustrate the point by a simplistic example. When you encounter deviations from ideality, some of which we mentioned above, simply take them into consideration arithmetically and logically to calculate a break-even point.

Example of Technique

Let's look at some illustrations and then calculate an example. We will present Figures 5.1 through 5.4 in succession and refer to them in order. Figure 5.1 is a simple graph consisting only of a straight horizontal line that represents fixed costs. Remember the definition of fixed costs: They are incurred regardless of whether we produce no product or quantities of product. Therefore, fixed costs appear as a horizontal straight line on the graph (zero slope).

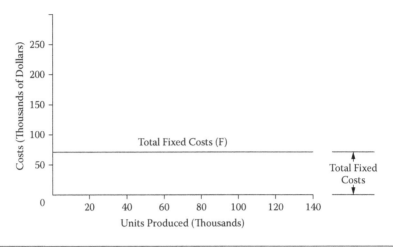

Figure 5.1

Figure 5.2 includes variable operating costs per item. A line with a positive slope indicates that the more units produced, the greater the operating costs. This is, in effect, our variable cost plot. Instead of starting it at the origin of the graph, we start it where the fixed costs line intersects the vertical axis. Remember that fixed costs are incurred before we ever produce an item. Therefore, the variable cost curve literally sits on top of the fixed curve because fixed costs plus variable costs equal total costs. By plotting the variable cost "curve" on top of the fixed cost line, the variable cost line automatically represents the total cost.

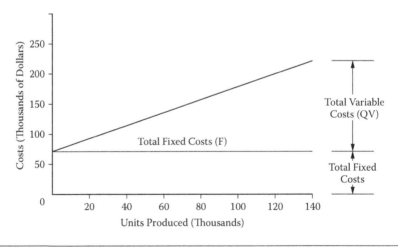

Figure 5.2

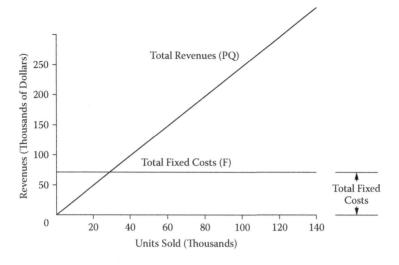

Figure 5.3

Now, using the vertical axis as dollars to indicate both costs and revenues, we will plot revenues. Figure 5.3 plots revenues. Essentially, this is a graphic representation of sales. If you sell one unit at $1, you plot $1. If you sell 3 units at $1 each, you plot $3, etc. Thus, you will have a straight line with a positive slope emanating from the origin of the graph. On Figure 5.4, we superimposed the revenue line with

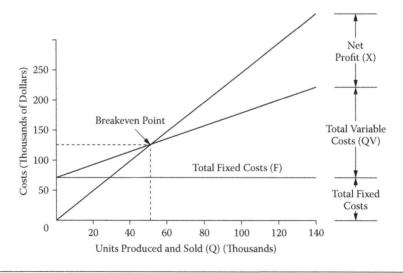

Figure 5.4

Table 5.1   Break-Even Point: Sales Revenue = Costs

BE =	Break-even point, volume, dollars
S =	Sales in dollars
Q =	Quantity produced and sold
VC =	Variable cost per unit
FC =	Fixed cost
P =	Price per unit

our cost lines and, as you might expect, the point of intersection is the break-even point, beyond which is profit.

Refer to Table 5.1. In this example we will use $3.00 as the selling price, $1.25 as the variable cost per item, and $70,000.00 as the fixed cost (Equation 5-1).

At the break-even point, sales revenue equals costs that represent the sum of fixed and variable costs. More simply, at the break-even point, sales equal costs. Sales equal the price per unit (selling price or P) multiplied by quantity sold (Q). At the break-even point, this is the fixed cost (FC) plus variable cost (VC) multiplied by quantity produced (Q), assuming Q is also the quantity sold.

Remember that moving a term from one side of an equation to the other simply changes its sign. We move the "variable cost × quantity sold" figure from the right side of the equation to the left to put Q in a position where we can factor it out as shown in the next step. Next we have quantity sold (Q) multiplied by the mathematical quanitity "price minus variable cost" as being equal to fixed cost. The equation is not ready to be solved yet; it needs more rearranging. Remember that when you divide one side of the equation by any number, you will not change the values represented as long as you divide the other side of the equation by the same number. Therefore, we can "clear" the left side by dividing that side by the (P − VC) arithmetic quantity but we must divide the right side by that same figure. The equation is now rearranged so that the quantity to sell to break even equals the fixed cost divided by the (P − VC) value. Our aim was to calculate the break-even point where sales equaled costs. The equation we derived indicates the quantity that must be sold to reach the break-even point.

$$\text{Sales} = \text{Costs}$$

$$P \times Q = FC + (VC \times Q)$$

$$P \times Q - (VC \times Q) = FC$$

$$Q \times (P - VC) = FC$$

$$Q = \frac{FC}{(P - VC)}$$

(5-1)

If fixed costs = $70,000.00, selling price = $3.00, and variable costs = $1.25:

$$3.00 \times Q = 70,000 + (1.25 \times Q)$$

$$3.00 \times Q - (1.25 \times Q) = 70,000$$

$$1.75Q = 70,000$$

$$Q = \frac{70,000}{1.75} = 40,000$$

The company must sell 40,000 units to break even. Sales beyond that number produce profit.

The calculation is not as cumbersome as it may seem. Remember, you know your fixed cost, selling price, and variable cost before you start production, so you can use this calculation early on in your manufacturing and selling predictions. In summary, Equation 5-1 calculates the quantity that must be produced and sold to break even. How many revenue dollars must you receive to break even? The answer is easy: multiply the quantity sold by the selling price.

Now let's use some numbers in our example. Assume our fixed cost equals $70,000 and the selling price of the product is $3.00; variable costs are $1.25 per item. Using Equation 5-1, we find that the break-even quantity is 40,000 units. In other words, 40,000 units must be sold to break even if we plan to bring this run of product to market. In reality, the company must sell many more than 40,000 items to make a profit. The initial sale of 40,000 takes the company from the loss range to the break-even point. The 40,001st item is sold for $3.00

of which $1.25 covers the variable cost. Since we have already met our fixed cost, we realize $1.75 profit.

Another (and simpler) way of looking at this issue is to again assume a $70,000 fixed cost and a $1.25 variable cost associated with each item sold. Therefore, we "make" $1.75 on each item sold, but we must first recover the fixed cost. To do so, we ask, "How many $1.75s are there in $70,000?" We divide $70,000 by $1.75 and again the result is 40,000 units. But remember that the company earns $1.75 on each unit sold beyond the first 40,000, and it's in business to make a profit, not simply break even.

How do we calculate the number of units that must be sold to produce a particular profit? Refer to Table 5.2. Use the basic break-even equation but let Q represent the quantity required to make a certain profit instead of the quantity needed to simply break even. Insert your desired profit on the right side of the equation. You will have to sell more units than required to break even, so Q (now called Q_p, where p indicates profit) equals the number of units that must be sold to earn the profit noted on the right side of the equation. If you want to make a profit of $50,000, insert that figure on the right side of the equation as you see in Table 5.2 and solve. You will have to sell 68,571 units to earn $50,000. In practice, you would round off the figure to 68,000 or 69,000. What sales revenue is required to achieve the $50,000 profit? Multiply the number of units by the price, or 68,571 × $3 = $205,713. You may round

Table 5.2   Profit beyond Break-Even Point

Suppose you desire a $50,000 profit:

$3.00 \times Q_p = 70,000 + (1.25 \times Q_p) + 50,000$

$(3.00 \times Q_p) - (1.25 \times Q_p) = 70,000 + 50,000$

$\$1.75 \times Q_p = 120,000$

$$Q_p = \frac{\$120,000}{\$1.75} = 68,571 \text{ units}$$

Dollar sales = $Q_p \times$ Price = $Q_p \times 3.00 = \$3.00 \times 68,571 = \$205,713$. To calculate the number of units to be sold to earn a certain profit, add the desired profit (p) to the right side of the equation.

that off to \$206,000 or \$210,000, but you have an exact figure to consider.

Managers must make decisions involving investments in equipment utilized for production. The investments involve fixed costs. Remember the list of items that fall in the fixed cost category. What motivates a manager to spend the money to increase fixed costs? He will *spend money to increase fixed costs when so doing will reduce variable costs.* This is basic. Why would you make a large expenditure if you would not gain an advantage from it? You might plan to replace antiquated equipment, thus reducing your variable cost. Replacing old equipment usually reduces other expenditures for variable costs.

Let's compare our example to a smaller investment in fixed costs and a higher investment in fixed costs. Remember, *the fixed costs and variable costs are simply for illustration. You must calculate the exact change in variable costs as a result of an investment in fixed costs based on specific figures that apply to your company.* The numbers here were selected to illustrate a point: when you increase fixed costs, you should reduce variable costs and vice versa.

We can calculate the break-even points for different combinations of fixed and variable costs. Refer to Table 5.3, which shows three different examples. Note that the selling price does not change. We calculated the number of units to break even and then multiplied that number by the \$3 selling price to determine sales revenue required to break even. The break-even point was reached sooner in the case where we reduced the fixed cost, and later where fixed costs were higher. Is this a contradiction to what we said above? No, it is not. Remember, we are aiming to earn a profit that is far beyond the break-even point.

Table 5.3 Changing Fixed and Variable Costs

	L	Ex	H
Fixed Costs	35,000	70,000	100,000
Variable Cost	1.60	1.25	1.00
Selling Price	3.00	3.00	3.00
Units	25,000	40,000	50,000
Dollar Revenue	75,000	120,000	150,000

L = lower fixed costs. Ex = figures from example. H = higher fixed costs.

In the case of higher fixed costs, the variable cost decreased to $1, yielding a $2 profit per item; the profit margin is greater beyond the break-even point. *When you increase your fixed cost, you should reduce your variable cost. You have a greater distance to go to reach your break-even point, but beyond that break-even point you achieve a greater profit per item throughout your profit range.* This is why you calculate the total market for your products, that is, the total quantity you anticipate selling in a particular period. Then you can determine what level of fixed cost investment you require.

Nonlinear Break-Even Analysis

An important consideration in discussing break-even analysis is that our example is very simplistic, such as variable costs remaining constant over the entire range of production. This is not always the case in reality. Variable costs will change with payments of overtime and bonuses and price breaks to customers, for example. The result of changes is a *nonlinear* break-even chart. At the break-even point in our basic linear example, profit was achieved along a straight line without incurring any losses. With nonlinear break-even, the line can transition from profit to loss, back to profit and again to loss. Refer to Figure 5.5 for an illustration.

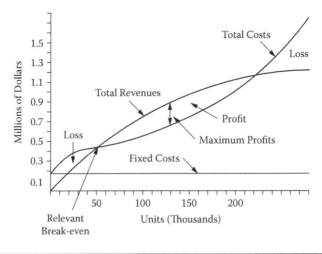

Figure 5.5 Nonlinear break-even progression.

Based on this nonlinear dynamic, a company may choose not to make or sell beyond a certain amount, thus cutting back total profit. In essence, this means not investing time and effort to achieve a decreased *margin*. When a nonlinear break-even chart indicates a narrow profit margin, you may decide to not pursue the small amount of profit per item or go beyond that to generate a greater profit margin. Of course, other considerations enter into the decision. For example, it is difficult to retain customers if you choose to run out of your product. No business decision is without impacts on many areas of the operation. This is why most manufacturers would continue to produce at the reduced margin—to satisfy their customers' needs.

6
STATISTICS
A Little Bit, Simply Explained

What managers need to make the proper decisions (along with the common sense and nerve required) is *information*. Today, many managers feel they need much more information than they receive. On occasion this is true, but in most cases today, the problem is not too little information. So much information is available that managers are overwhelmed, although they usually say they have a lot of data to sort. The fact is that management information service (MIS) groups provide an overabundance of data. Piles of computer printouts on office desks are common sights. Companies also store an abundance of data on their main computer drives and servers. A successful manager knows what data to extract from the reams of data available in print or stored in computer memory.

Comparing the reams of computer printouts to a smorgasbord dinner is a good analogy. You don't eat everything you see at a smorgasbord; you choose a combination of food and beverage that suits your needs at the moment. If you walk down a smorgasbord line, you may choose a roast beef sandwich, a little salad, and perhaps a diet soda. Someone else will make other choices. The person who tries to select everything appears not to know what his best choices are.

The same principal applies to information in business. You work most efficiently when you can select a combination of information that fills your needs at that moment. If you have information that may be used by other people, shift it to them for their use, especially if they work for you. In summary, knowing what the necessary information is and how to use it works far more efficiently than having an abundance of information that is not sorted properly and is thus not useful.

Cause and Effect

In sorting data, it is important to realize if there is a cause and effect relationship between the data. This is referred to as a causal relationship. This is not to be confused with a casual relationship where X only causes Y to occur once in a while. When X regularly causes Y then it's a causal relationship; X and Y represent cause and effect. Note the difference in the two words—causal and casual.

Here is an example of how some top managers can be misled. Convenience stores throughout the world belong to large chains or are small independent operations. A large chain in the Middle Atlantic section of the United States recently installed sandwich counters where they prepare take-out sandwiches in the belief that this measure will increase sales.

During visits to this store, I observed that the sandwiches are made to order and therefore take several minutes to prepare. The average sandwich price is about $7. The average shopping order is $14 to $18 for purchases like milk, orange juice, cheese, etc. Rarely did a customer buy a take-out sandwich and walk through the aisles to find other items. Customers who bought sandwiches and beverages usually left the store. The chain did not hire extra staff for the sandwich counter. Cashiers were required to check customers out and make sandwiches. Sandwich customers were asked what kind of cheese they wanted, whether they wanted red or green peppers, onions, mushrooms, etc. Customers waiting at the cashier station to buy other items frequently returned the items to the shelves or simply put them on the counter and left the store.

In a discussion with a regional supervisor, I asked how the sandwich counter was doing and the reply was that it boosted sales about 1 to 1.5%. The supervisor thought the installation of sandwich counters was good because, for unexplained reasons, regular store sales were down about 3%. In fact, the sandwich counter *caused* regular sales to decrease. A computer printout and a mountain of data would not have revealed that fact. Of course the supervisor believes the sandwich counter was a good idea because he read the data. However, the activity at the store clearly revealed a cause-and-effect relationship that should have led to a decision to hire more help or close the sandwich counter. This shows how good managers must *see what's actually going on* in their operations instead of only reading data.

Another example is a case where a salesperson for an imaginary product plots the number of customer calls against the volume of sales made. If doubling his number of calls doubles his sales and thus doubles his income, we can assume a cause-and-effect relationship, but only if no third event is put into motion at the same time. For example, a television advertising campaign launched when the salesperson doubled his calls must also be considered a factor. The increased number of sales calls can be credited with the sales increase only if all other factors remained constant. Whenever you compare data, you must ask whether one set of data causes another set or whether the second set was caused by a third event or factor.

Standard Deviation and Normal Curve

Figure 6.1 shows a normal curve representing a normal distribution. This is also known as a Gaussian (bell-shaped) curve representing a Gaussian (bell-shaped) distribution. This type of distribution is named for Carl Friedrich Gauss, a German mathematician and physicist.

Examination of the curve shows an equal number of values to the right and to the left of the median. In this case, median and average are the same. More will be said about this type of distribution below.

The question arises as to the type of distribution not represented by a bell-shaped curve. This different-from-normal distribution is called skewed distribution. Figure 6.2 shows a distribution skewed to the left.

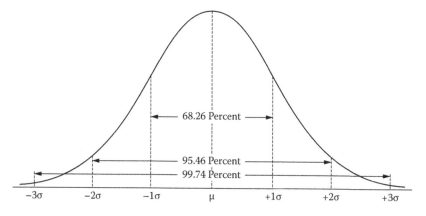

Figure 6.1   Normal, bell-shaped, or Gaussian curve.

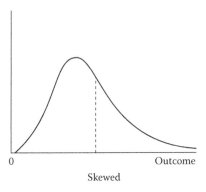

Figure 6.2   Skewed distribution.

Other distributions can be skewed to the right or left, that is, show predominance on the right or left side or display higher values. This type of distribution is beyond the scope of this chapter; we will discuss only normal distribution.

We will define a standard deviation represented by the Greek letter sigma σ. Before we learn to calculate the standard deviation, it is important to know what it means. Referring again to Figure 6.1, we see that the center or median line represents the average value of a series of measurements (observations). When we plot the values and see that a normal distribution is obtained, we can then calculate a value called variance, σ^2, from which we take the square root and calculate the standard deviation or σ. The standard deviation is the value within which 68.3% of all values for this given set of data will fall, i.e., when you calculate a standard deviation and then from the average calculate a range of ±1 standard deviation, 68.3% of all the values represented by the population (total from which your selected number of observations was made) will fall within that range. Thus, if you made 1,000 observations, 683 of them would fall in that range. In a population of 1,000,000, then 683,000 would be within that range. Extending the range to 2 σ, which is really ±2 σ, broadens the area under the curve about which we are speaking and a far greater percentage (95.4%) of the population will fall into this new range defined as ±2 σ. We see that ±3 σ represents 99.7% of the total population.

The ability to predict the range within which a percentage of values in a population exists is a very important implication of the standard deviation and the standard deviation range.

Before we can calculate a standard deviation, we must calculate the variance on which it is based. The standard deviation is the square root of the variance. We will use a very simplified example. Assume you manufacture bottles of shampoo. Each bottle should contain 20 ounces of product. The plastic bottle can hold 24 ounces, to provide "head space" for expansion of the product when subjected to heat during shipment, to allow for a slight overfill, and to give the impression that the bottle contains more than it does. There are a number of reasons why 20 ounces of material will be packed in a 24 ounce bottle. The nature of your manufacturing and filling processes means one bottle may contain less than 20 ounces and another bottle may contain more. We will consider any bottle over 20.0 ounces an overfill and any bottle under 20.0 ounces an underfill.

In this simplified example, we will take only 20 observations (samples) to simplify the math. In reality, if you are filling 100 bottles per minute (6,000 per hour), you might measure 1 sample per minute (60 per hour). The 20 samples for our example will come from a population of many thousands. The sample bottles will be taken at random time intervals and the volume of shampoo contained will be measured for each bottle. We will assume a normal distribution here. Table 6.1 shows measurements of the contents.

Variance equals the sum of the squares of the deviations of each sample reading from the average sample reading, divided by 1 fewer than the number of observations:

$$\text{variance} = \sigma^2 = \frac{\Sigma\left(\Delta^2\right)}{n-1} \tag{6-1}$$

To find the standard deviation, you simply calculate the square root of the variance. The variance is expressed as σ^2 (sigma squared) and its square root is σ (sigma or the standard deviation) expressed as:

$$\text{standard deviation} = \sqrt{\sigma^2} = \sigma = \sqrt{\frac{\Sigma\left(\Delta^2\right)}{n-1}} \tag{6-2}$$

We rounded to the first decimal for illustration purposes. In reality, you may use any number of decimals appropriate for your process. Our standard deviation is 0.7.

Table 6.1   Variances of Contents of 20
Samples of 20-Ounce Shampoo Bottles

OBSERVATION (OUNCES)	Δ	Δ^2
19.8	−0.2	.04
19.6	−0.4	.16
20.1	+0.1	.01
21.0	+1.0	1.0
19.8	−0.2	.04
20.3	+0.3	.09
21.2	+1.2	1.44
21.0	+1.0	1.0
19.0	−1.0	1.0
18.8	−1.2	1.44
20.0	0	0
20.0	0	0
19.8	−0.2	.04
19.9	−0.1	.01
19.5	−0.5	.25
20.6	+0.6	.36
20.3	+0.3	.09
19.7	−0.3	.09
18.7	−1.3	1.69
20.8	+0.8	<u>0.64</u>
		9.43
		$= \Sigma \, \Delta^2$

$$\sigma^2 = \frac{9.43}{(20-1)} = .4963$$

$$\sqrt{\sigma^2} = \sigma = .70$$

Before we discuss the significance of a sigma range, we define the one standard deviation range as ±1 standard deviation from the average. In our case, the average is 20.0. Since the standard deviation of our example is 0.7, the ±1 standard deviation range (or one standard deviation range) is 20 ± 0.7 or 19.3 to 20.7 ounces. As shown in Figure 6.1, 68.3% of our data will fall within that range. In fact, in any normal distribution, 68.3% of all the values obtained will fall within the ±1 standard deviation range.

The two standard deviation range (2 sigma or 2 σ) defines the area within which 95.4% of all values will fall. In our example, two standard deviations are expressed as 2 × 0.7 = 1.4. Thus, our two standard deviation range = 20 ± 1.4 or 18.6 to 21.4 ounces. The three standard deviation value is calculated the same way (3 × 0.7 = equals 2.1) and the 3 σ range based on ±2.1 is 17.9 to 22.1 ounces. Therefore, 99.7% of all the values obtained from our process will fall between 17.9 and 22.1 ounces. If any part of the process changes in any way, the distribution may deviate from normal or produce a different average. If no changes occur, we can expect the values to fall within the predicted ranges.

The reason for squaring measurements is to provide a true measure of the extent of deviation from the desired amount or value. Without squaring, the underfills in our sample would negate the overfills in the arithmetic calculation and the result would be incorrect, or exact negation would indicate that the fills were perfect, despite the evidence of underfills and overfills.

Thus the squaring, totaling as positive numbers, and calculating the square root precludes such errors and yields an accurate indication.

You may note a uniform but narrow distribution that indicates consistency, but if the average is offset from what you want it to be, you don't have accuracy. You must look at the entire distribution to include the average value for accuracy and the standard deviation for consistency. You want both accuracy and consistency, otherwise you may have to adjust your process. There's more about this below.

Standard Deviation and Width of Distribution

The width of the peak is an important consideration in a normal distribution. Our distribution indicated that our average was on target

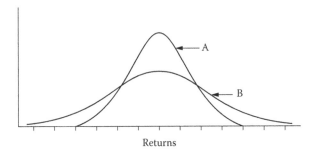

Returns

Figure 6.3 Probability Distributions; A and B.

to our desired average. In addition, the standard deviation appeared reasonably good, but the important issue is whether the result suits your process.

Let's look at possibilities. Refer to Figure 6.3. We see for Project B (arrow) that the desired average is what we want. However, the distribution, while still normal, is very broad. This type of distribution will have a large deviation associated with it, perhaps a standard deviation of 2 or 3 or 4. A standard deviation of 4 would yield a one standard deviation range of 20 ± 4 (16 to 24) which is undesirable. The average is near or exactly as desired but the distribution, while normal, is very broad, as evidenced by a high σ or standard deviation value.

The next case is illustrated in Figure 6.3 Project A where the distribution is narrow. It is a normal distribution with a good, i.e. small, standard deviation figure. However, imagine that the average is not what we want it to be. For example, using our case, we may have a standard deviation of only 0.2 or 0.3, which would give us the narrow distribution, but is different than as shown in the figure. We may want 20 as a target value and have a peak around 18. That means we have a tightly controlled but inaccurate system. You can visualize that curve A would be shifted to the left. In a tightly controlled process, you want the average to be at the value you specified and the standard deviation to be small, indicating a narrow range. When both of these aspects meet your need, you have a good distribution.

Z Value

Z value is a representation of the number of standard deviations away from the mean or average of a given value. Some books include complex formulas to calculate it. In our example of filling shampoo bottles (average of 20, standard deviation of 0.7), if we select any isolated value and find it is one standard deviation away from our average, that is, a value of 19.3 to 20.7, it has a Z value of 1. For another example of the same process, assume a value of 18.95, which is 1.05 away from our average. Since our standard deviation is 0.7 and the deviation from the average is 1.05, we divide 1.05 by 0.7 and the result (Z value) is 1.5.

What function does a Z value serve? If you are comparing two different but similar systems (for example, two separate assembly lines making the same product in a production area), one theory is to compare any given value to the mean of that system by computing how many standard deviations that value is away from the mean. Both production lines can have the same average and somewhat different standard deviations. You don't want that, but the situation may be acceptable at a given point in time. Maybe neither production line has indicated it should be shut down for repairs, but one shows a greater standard deviation. Comparing an observation or sample from one line to an observation or sample from the other line may show a significant difference if each result is calculated as a percentage difference from the average. However, when compared by the Z value (number of standard deviations from the average), the results may be very similar.

For example, if two assembly lines show averages of 20 but one has a standard deviation of 0.7 and one has a standard deviation of 1.0, a value of 19.3 for the first one represents the same distance away from the average as does a value of 19 on the second line from its average when compared by Z values, because both lines are one standard deviation away from their own averages and thus both are performing well with respect to the "efficiency" of their systems. If the comparison was made on a percentage basis, the first value would be 0.7/20 or 3.5% away from the average, and the second line sample would be 1/20 or 5% away from the average.

The Z value simply represents another way to look at a system. When you evaluate a process or system that has a normal (Gaussian or bell-shaped) distribution, the average, standard deviation (σ), and Z value allow you to analyze different aspects of the process.

"Statistics are like bikinis; what they reveal is interesting—what they conceal is vital."

7

GRAPHS, CHARTS, AND EQUATIONS

The title of this chapter could justifiably be "Miscellaneous Arithmetic and Proper Presentation Skills." The reason for including this material is that most business decisions involve numbers of one kind or another. Arithmetic combined with common sense and judgment leads to effective business decisions. This does not diminish the importance of advanced mathematics like differential equations, but most business situations a manager faces do not require higher mathematics. Hopefully this material will help you focus on the decision making process.

When you need data to make a decision or a business evaluation, you should ask yourself certain questions:

- What am I trying to determine?
- What data do I need?
  - What do I already have?
  - What do I still need?
- How do I obtain this data?
- What does it mean?
- What is the best way to look at this data to interpret it properly?
- How should I present this data to others to convince them of my views?

Essentially, most of the data evaluated in business involves some or all of the questions presented above. At times you may view presentations of data and realize it has significance but you don't see what it is. If the significance is not clear, the presentation is not effective.

When you are presented with data that appears unclear to you, present the numerical information to yourself in a different way. A case in point is choosing incorrect scales for the axes of graphs; the dots representing the individual points seem to fall far away from the line drawn to represent the trend illustrated by the points. Sometimes the converse is true; every point seems to fall right on the line when in reality you know that that could not be the case. Plot the data differently and possibly some facts will almost jump out at you—facts that were present but not apparent in the original presentation form.

Another pitfall is presenting data on a line chart that could have been better represented on a bar chart. The numbers may appear to be significant but the presenter doesn't deliver them in a fashion that you can readily understand. If you ever presented data in such a way that your audience had difficulty understanding what you meant, you now know why they gave you incredulous stares. Paying careful attention to *how data is presented* can ensure that you convey your message properly to your audience; as a side benefit, this can further your career.

Think about it. How can people evaluate you or your information if they don't understand what you are trying to say? When people can understand your information, they know your position and will listen to you. This does not mean they will always agree with you, but they will pay more attention to you than when they can't understand you.

Visual Means of Presenting Data

Today, computer graphics allow managers impressive methods of presenting data. Available computer programs can assist you in delivering your message very efficiently. However, don't make the mistake of getting carried away with computer programs. Know how to use them to present what you want to present. The two classic cases of misuse are:

- Minimal data presented in numerous ways
- Much data presented in so many ways that the result is overwhelming

The person presenting the little bit of data didn't know how to present it, got carried away with the computer program, and forgot the message he was trying to convey. His report would be described as *a lot of style but no substance.*

The presenter in the latter case was not sure of the best way to present his data, and therefore presented the information in every way he knew, thus overwhelming the audience. You can present data two or three different ways if your audience includes various disciplines (e.g., production staff, scientists, salespeople) and you want to convey clear information based on what these types of people feel most comfortable reading. This is vastly different from confusion on a presenter's part to the point where information is presented again with *a lot of style but no substance* because the substance got lost in the mountain of data.

Text Charts

Figure 7.1 is a text chart used to convey information. You must follow certain rules if you want people to read and understand the information in a text chart:

- Use large print that can be read easily.
- Use only a few words. Don't try to get a very detailed message across on one slide or transparency. You can use additional slides. If three or more are required to tell your story, use that many.
- Try to make only a few main points; don't try to squeeze too many points of view on one chart. Again, you can use several charts to illustrate different points. It is easier for readers to comprehend one point per chart (which is what you want them to do).
- Before you prepare any chart, ask yourself "What am I trying to say?" and "To whom am I trying to say it?" After you answer both questions you are well on your way to preparing an effective chart.

Example of Text Chart

Bananas Sold	
Month	Tons
January	34
February	43
March	58
April	60
May	52
June	37
July	26
August	22
September	25
October	29
November	30
December	32

Figure 7.1 Text chart.

Line Charts

Figure 7.2 is a line chart. The horizontal axis is called the X axis and the vertical axis is labeled the Y axis. We refer to X as the *independent variable* and the calculated values of Y as the *dependent variable*. For example, if in the equation Y = 2X we set the independent variable X equal to 5, then the dependent variable is 2 × 5 which is 10. In this case, the value of Y depends on the value of X. Specifically, it is twice the value of X in accordance with the equation Y = 2X.

Similarly, if Y = 4X and the independent variable X is 5, the dependent variable Y is equal to 4 × 5 or 20. The dependent variable Y "depends on" and is related to the value of the independent variable X as defined by the particular equation.

When preparing a line chart, you plot a series of points (each defined by a pair of X and Y values). Then you "regress," which simply means that you draw a line connecting the dots. This technique is sometimes called "regression analysis."

A word of caution: if you draw straight lines from dot to dot, you will have created a strange graph that will not represent the trend that you are trying to portray. If you have determined the proper number of points, spaced the proper distance apart, you should draw a line that indicates a trend of the point sets and will represent a much neater presentation. Figure 7.2 shows the dot-to-dot connection. Picture it

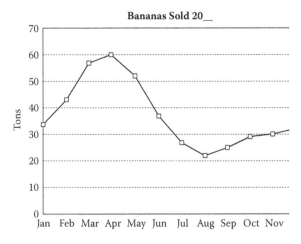

Figure 7.2 Line chart.

(or sketch it with a pencil) "smoothed out" with more points such as weekly values. This would provide 52 points instead of the 12 shown. If your points are too far apart to draw a straight line or smooth curve through them by "rounding," you may not have a relationship to plot. You must have a real relationship between the X and Y values to plot a reasonably straight line or curve.

Bar Charts

Figure 7.3 shows a bar chart presentation. Bar charts are used to present comparisons of individual accomplishments at distinct periods of time. Of course, you can say that about most graphs, but let's illustrate the point. A typical example would be a presentation of sales revenue on the Y (vertical) axis over a year on the X (horizontal) axis. The result is a pictorial representation of the activity (positive or negative) compared over time.

Presenting such data on a dot type plot with a curve (as in Figure 7.2) the result would be reasonably readable, but in the bar chart form, the changes are more readily apparent. Use some paper, a pen, and a thick felt marker to sketch a bar chart showing data you want to present and critically review the result. If you use markers of different colors, you can develop a very creative plot. Alternatively, various computerized presentation programs are available.

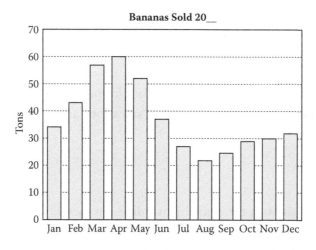

Figure 7.3 Bar chart.

Table 7.1 Sales by Division

DIVISION	SALES (MILLIONS OF DOLLARS)	SALES (% OF TOTAL)
A	100	40
B	70	28
C	30	12
D	<u>50</u>	<u>20</u>
Total	250	100

In a cumulative bar chart, one bar is placed on top of, offset from, or added to another bar at the same position on the X axis. In black and white, this is achieved by bars of various shadings. In color presentations, different facts are represented by different colors. For example, you could present the data for sales and the data for profits on the same chart by offsetting the different color bars slightly. Remember that you have only a small width across the paper on the X axis in which to portray a time frame. You could represent sales by a vertical bar and add a bar representing profits immediately adjacent to the right. This allows an audience to see a performance trend and determine whether profits did or did not parallel sales over time.

Another application of a cumulative bar presentation is to present the sales from different divisions or departments on a single chart. You may choose to construct your own offset bar chart representing the sales and profits of different divisions using the data in Table 7.1, or use your own real data to view areas of performance of your own business.

Be careful not to include too much information on a single chart. It will appear to your audience as a "snow job" and will be counterproductive.

Pie Charts

Figure 7.4 shows a pie chart in two different views. This is the preferred form of presentation when the individual data components must be equated to the whole—the total of all your data will be considered to equal 100% and the individual parts will be represented by their

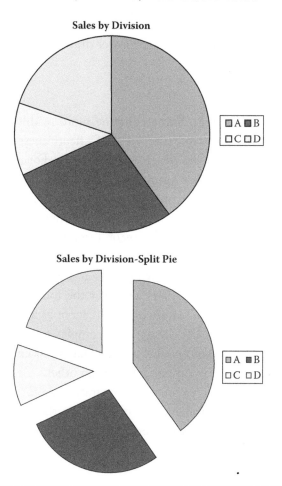

Figure 7.4   Pie charts illustrating Table 7.1 data.

respective percentages. This does not require the use of percentage figures in your chart. You can use the numbers representing your data as we did for sales in our previous figures. It simply means that you are comparing individual numbers to the entire total.

You can plot the sections of a pie chart (in this case four) by placing the exact sales figures in the chart, each representing a wedge of the pie, and note at the bottom that the sales total $250 million. Another method is to list each sales division by its respective percent of the 100% total and note at the bottom that the figures represent percentages of total sales for the period. To show a particular division's performance and make it stand out, one technique is to move the wedge representing that division slightly out from the center. This is called a "split pie chart" and is shown in the lower drawing of Figure 7.4.

Combination Charts

Charts can be combined. Some combine more readily than others, both aesthetically and from the view of effectiveness. Experiment with combinations and see which works for you. For example, a bar chart could illustrate sales figures and a line chart could represent profits from sales and they could be superimposed. A third relationship could be included. The first graph, a bar chart, would show the relationship of sales to years. The second graph, a line chart, would show the relationships of profits for the same years. The combined graph would, in addition to showing sales and profits, illustrate their relationships for individual years and over the total time span. This type of chart can aid your evaluation and serve as a presentation to others. Again, do not make the material complex to the point of confusing your audience. Your goal is to show data in its entirety and the relationships of the data components to each other.

Another technique is to present a separate scale for the Y axis on the right side of the graph and to offset it from the scale on the left. In effect you would have two superimposed graphs with a common X axis and different Y axes.

Summary

Various types of graphs and charts are available for presentations. A common version is the organization chart using solid lines to show reporting relationships, for example, directors reporting to vice presidents who in turn report to the president, etc. Possible innovations are limited only by your imagination.

To select a proper presentation style for data, you should determine what you want to say and to whom you want to say it. This means defining your audience. Be aware of their backgrounds and tailor your presentation to what they need to know about the subject matter you want to discuss.

The next step is a rough sketch of the presentation you would like to make, using a pen and felt tip markers on paper to see how it will look.

Many people make dull presentations because they use the same type of graph over and over without analyzing whether the format presents the data clearly. Charts and graphs are intended to clarify information you want to convey, not to distract from it or confuse viewers. If you take the time to determine the best way to present information, your audience will understand what you are trying to convey and you will be pleased with your presentations.

8

MANUFACTURING

If you are a scientist—and this is especially applicable if you are a research scientist—you may ask why you should care about manufacturing functions. The answer is important to you. If you design a product that cannot be made economically from a manufacturing, financial, or marketing point of view, your company doesn't have a product and you may not have a job. That should be sufficient motivation to learn about manufacturing. If you are involved in quality control or technical services, you must know how your product was, is, or will be manufactured so that you can work effectively. You should also know what types of processes are run in your plant so that a new product you design can be produced on existing equipment. Even if you have the luxury of designing a product and determining the equipment to be purchased to manufacture it, you should still understand the general aspects of manufacturing.

Over the years, brilliant product development people have designed new products in laboratories only to find out that the products could not be produced economically. Conversely, if your job is to develop new products, don't consider economics initially because it will restrict your imagination. If you are a researcher, forget about the economics until you have developed an initial product or process. Then, as you refine the initial version to the prototype state, you can consider economic factors. Economics is not a factor early in the creative process, but it becomes an important consideration for production planning. Some questions to ask yourself when designing a new product are:

- Can it be made?
- Can it be made economically?*
- Can it be made of materials that are readily available?

---

* Define "economically" for your operation. Work with actual dollar values, not vague terms like "too costly."

- Will it sell in the marketplace?
- What skills do people need to manufacture it?
- Can our existing equipment produce it or do we need new equipment?
- Can a suitable quality level be achieved consistently?
- Can we test it accurately and consistently for quality?
- Will it meet regulatory requirements, i.e., is it environmentally clean, etc.?
- What other considerations are relevant to this product?

Types of Production Systems

The three types of production systems are job shop, batch, and continuous operations.

Job Shop Production

Each customer order represents an individual job. Each product is customized for each customer. Production is scheduled based on whether the necessary parts are in stock or must be ordered for a job. Examples of job shops are automobile repair and hair styling businesses.

Batch Production

This type of production involves making several items from raw materials at one time. Each item has its own characteristic identification or lot number. Each batch or lot of final product is set aside for shipping and a new batch is started. Pharmaceutical products are examples of batch production. Each batch receives a lot number or alternatively several batches may be combined within an individual lot number. The lot identification number, usually composed of letters and numbers, will identify to the manufacturer the plant at which the material was manufactured and the date of manufacture. Some lot identification numbers also include the time of day and the production line on which the batch was produced.

Continuous Production

As the name implies, production is continuous and raw materials are replaced as used. This type of operation requires more effort to keep track of the lots and identification numbers of the raw materials because new identification numbers for raw materials must be incorporated into the flow of the system. Additionally, a lot number is assigned to every X number of items produced by a line. This is done for tracking purposes to benefit both the consumer and the manufacturer.

The manufacturer determines the size of a lot. The number must be large enough to accommodate many individual items (hundreds, thousands, or even millions) but not so large as to cover several lots of different components. *Traceability* of product components is important if a problem arises after the product reaches the market. Large paper rolls are examples of continuous manufactured products. The ingredients are continuously added as the mixture moves along the production line.

Combination Production

In reality, many manufacturing processes combine batch and continuous operations. For example, in tire manufacturing, a batch of compounded rubber formulation is produced and then the batch is used to make many tires. The tires are continually produced in molds in rapid succession; each tire is molded for several minutes. The important issue for a manufacturer is to ensure *traceability* of your ingredients.

Why do you need traceability of ingredients that constitute a final product? If a problem arises and you can trace it to a lot of raw material used in your product, you can correct the problem and prevent recurrence. If there is a problem and no difference in ingredient quality is detected, perhaps a problem occurred in the production process. If a product differs in quality, a raw material (content or quality) or a step in the process may have varied. Determine what differed from earlier production and correct the deficiency.

Inputs to Production Planning Systems

When management plans production of a new product, it must consider certain factors:

- Raw material availability
- Suppliers that can deliver proper quality on time

- Market demand
- Economic conditions such as stable material and labor costs
- Competitors
- Relevant legal and regulatory requirements for ingredients and product
- Available work force with required knowledge and training
- Inventory levels
- Sufficient work force and space to handle production activities
- Sufficient equipment and space to handle production activities
- Distributors and outlets or capability for selling directly to customers

Key Personnel

The individual workers on the line, their supervisors, and foremen play important roles, as do inspectors and shippers. Certain other positions are also key and may be overlooked by non-production areas. The plant manager "runs the plant," and is responsible for all activities inside the plant. Two other important positions are the planner and the scheduler. In smaller operations, one person may handle both planning and scheduling. The line between production planning and production scheduling is extremely narrow. Generally speaking, next week's production is the responsibility of the scheduler. Determining what will be produced three weeks or more from now becomes the planner's responsibility.

When one or two people perform these functions, we will call the function "planning" to keep the principles simple. The planner must understand the production processes, raw materials required, when those materials will be received, personnel and equipment available, and potential problems. How can you plan production if you don't know the product and the system? The production planner must understand all these issues to achieve efficient production. This is why knowledgeable planners are often promoted to plant managers.

Why should a researcher care about production planning? After your product successfully goes through the pilot plant stage and is set for its first production run, the planner will manage the initial process and handle subsequent planning and scheduling. You should develop a relationship with the planner and arrange to watch the initial product run. This will enable you to note potential problems before they become major ones. You want your new product to succeed and the first step is ensuring an efficient initial production run. The production planner can help you achieve that.

Another important consideration for you as the technical person, and for the plant manager, the planner, the scheduler, and others in the production area is a solid understanding of the production process. You should know the chronological order of the steps and also know which step is *the most expensive, the next most expensive, and so on*. Why is this important? You may have a good product but the economics may not be favorable. If you are familiar with the costs of each step in the process, you can direct your activities toward the most costly steps and possibly modify them to bring costs in line faster and get your product to market successfully.

Total Quality Management (TQM)

TQM is not a new concept; it has been around a long time. The concept under the TQM name has made a lot of money for consultants over the years. The same or similar quality principles are repackaged under a new name about every 25 years and high fees are extracted from company managers who want TQM or the latest repackaging of it.

In brief, TQM enhances quality consciousness and attention at every step of production—from initial design of the product, to set-up of the system, receipt of the raw materials, manufacturing, final packaging, shipping of the product, and to products in the customer's possession. In "the old days," manufacturing was a fairly simple process and at the end of the line inspectors sorted good products from the bad. Tightening quality control procedures simply meant instructing inspectors to look more stringently at the products and sort more tightly. This meant sorting out good product on occasion, but manufacturers were willing to incur that cost to increase quality level. TQM theoretically allows a business to produce only good product; it has little or no undesirable product to discard or recycle. The quality concept exists beyond manufacturing into administrative and other areas. Because overall quality is higher, fewer inspectors are needed and less material is rejected or reworked. Companies spend less to achieve higher quality with the TQM concept than they spent to discard poor product. It seems reasonable that it costs less to make satisfactory products than to make them at a low quality level and reject a percentage of production.

While quality terminology continuously changes, the essence of the concept remains the same: *Make the right thing the right way the first time and every time.* Implementing TQM in your company can be done easily and inexpensively by paying attention to detail; the alternative is an expensive consulting fee.

Other production systems merit mention here. Lean manufacturing or lean production (often called simply "lean") is a theory of production that considers expenditures of resources for any reason other than the creation of value for presumed customers to be wasteful and thus targets for elimination. More basically, lean means "more value with less work." The system is said to have been derived from the Toyota Production System (TPS). "Lean" in this context means "no waste."

Other well known systems include Reliability Centered Maintenance (RCM), Total Productive Maintenance (TPM), Quick Response Manufacturing (QRM), and the Theory of Constraints (TOC).* All these methods aim to achieve high quality in an economic manner. They simply represent different roads to the same destination.

Just-in-Time (JIT) Inventory

In a JIT inventory control procedure, the necessary components or materials arrive in the production area "just in time" for assembly into the final product. This eliminates large storage costs. Depending on the product manufactured, JIT can apply to materials coming from your warehouse to the production area when needed or it may refer to large items (tractors or earth moving equipment) that arrive at your plant from suppliers just in time for your production assembly.

---

* Chemists will recognize TOC as meaning Total Organic Carbon. Various disciplines use their own sets of initials as a type of shorthand for terms they use frequently. Always know what acronyms represent to avoid confusion about terminology.

Let's look first at the three types of inventory costs:

- Ordering costs
- Carrying costs
- Costs of running out

Ordering costs remain constant per order. Carrying costs are incurred to store parts in inventory and will vary by number of parts stored. If you order a few parts frequently, storage cost is minimal but ordering costs are large, since you order many times. Conversely, if you place a few large orders, your ordering costs are minimized but your carrying costs increase because you store large quantities of items. One goes up, the other goes down.

Economic order quantity (EOQ) calculates the total of ordering and carrying costs to determine a minimum cost of ordering. For example, when you calculate so many parts per order and how many you will use in a year, you can calculate the number of orders per year per part. Ordering fewer parts more frequently or ordering larger quantities less frequently would produce different results. When the results are plotted, the lowest total represents the EOQ—the level of inventory that minimizes the total of holding and ordering costs.

The "costs of running out" are not always taken into consideration and they may be very high. Many managers don't think about them. Also, these costs are approximations and may be neglected because they are not exact. The cost of running out of an inventory item in a retail store does not only lead to the loss of that sale. A customer who goes to another store to make the purchase may be swayed over to becoming a regular customer there. The customer may also tell other people that the first store did not stock a particular item. The main point here is that the first store didn't lose one sale. It may have lost a lot more.

If you run out of an inventory part on a production line, you must stop the entire line. Here is where JIT forces you to walk a tightrope. You can minimize your inventory costs by having materials arrive from your supplier or warehouse just in time. As long as they arrive just in time, production continues. If the inventory doesn't arrive in time, your production will stop, and cost you a lot of money to run your plant without producing saleable product.

Keep in mind:

Speed
Quality
Price
(Pick any 2)

Assume you want a supplier to deliver a part or shipment to you exactly when you need it and no earlier. You are not the supplier's only customer so the supplier must change his schedule to accommodate your requirements and thus modify shipments to his other customers. He is not going to do this at no charge. The JIT concept is good in theory, but don't assume that you will not have to pay for the service. While it may work well for you, it is very idealistic and can result in serious problems if supplies do not arrive when needed.

Types of Inventories

It important to mention the three types of inventory on hand in most production.

- Raw materials
- Work in process
- Finished goods

Every production system involves parts or ingredients in storage waiting to be fed into the assembly line, work in process along the assembly line, and finished, packaged product awaiting shipment to customers. Accountants need figures for raw materials, work in process, and finished product so that they can continually track company assets. Production people must ensure that work flows efficiently through assembly lines. If you consider your assembly line not simply as a process, but from the viewpoint of raw materials, work in process, and product for shipping, you will have a good perspective of plant dynamics. You should also determine parameters to be tested at various stages of production, including the finished product, to ensure proper quality.

If you are conducting a quality audit of your plant, start by reviewing the organization chart (or table of organization) that lists staff and their areas of responsibility, and then follow the trail of your product from the receipt of raw materials through work in progress to finished goods. Assure that each area is doing its assigned job and that the work flows as it should. This technique is faster and more efficient than more complex procedures.

9

ACCOUNTING

Why should a technical manager know about accounting functions? Answer that question with a few other questions and you
may understand.

- How is your department listed in the ledger books?
- If you are a research manager, is your operation listed as
  overhead?
- Do you receive a fair share of the budget or should your
  department receive more money?
- If you knew more about company revenue and expenses, could
  you increase allocations to your department?
- Do you know how the budget is distributed to departments,
  i.e., what criteria determine who gets what?

If you cannot answer these questions, you may want to learn more
about your company's accounting function. In Chapter 4, we covered finance. Recall that a financial manager makes many investment
decisions relevant to the continuation and growth of a firm based on
information he receives from accounting or another in-house source.
The accounting department tracks inflows and outflows of money
through the company and maintains records of its *sources and uses,* that
is, *how it came in and how it went out.* In brief, the financial manager
decides or advises on how to spend the money; the accounting department keeps records of it. That admittedly oversimplified description is
appropriate for our use now.

Accounting and Bookkeeping

Bookkeeping is the process of systematically recording basic accounting data such as revenues from the sales of products and expenses
from operations such as rents, wages, cost of goods sold, and more. In

essence, bookkeeping is the recording of money coming in and going out. The function of accounting is to maintain financial information and make it readily available to management for use in making financial decisions. Accounting principles determine which transactions are recorded where. Accountants prepare financial statements for managers who evaluate them and use the data to make decisions.

Budgets

Sales forecasts (see Chapter 3) determine budgets. The forecasts result from the combined efforts of the sales and marketing departments. Think about it with regard to your personal financial planning. If you want to take an expensive vacation next year, you must "forecast" your anticipated income between now and then. Will you get a raise? Will you get a bonus? Will you still have a job? Based on what you believe about your current job, you will estimate your next year's income and then you will determine whether you can incur the expense of the exotic vacation. You follow this process for any major expenditure like a new car or college for your children.

The forecasting principle also applies to business. To determine what you can spend on projects you want to implement next year, you must anticipate your income (in this case the profit from sales revenue allocated to your department). *The sales forecast is the basis for the budget.* The accounting group tracks actual cash inflows and outflows. The financial manager determines how revenue will be invested to ensure sufficient cash receipts in the future.

Accounting Functions

Accounting provides information on the firm's financial condition to various interested groups:

- The management of the firm
- The company's stockholders and the general public (if it is a public corporation)
- The Internal Revenue Service

Information made available to the public is in the form of an annual report. Large corporations usually prepare elaborate annual reports and also make them available on company websites. The purpose of an annual report is to let the public know about the company's performance and stimulate investment by convincing the general public to buy the company's stock. A letter from the chairman of the board or president of the company included in an annual report will reflect the philosophy of the company. Before you read that, turn to the auditor's statement. An auditor is an independent reviewer, usually an accounting firm, hired by the company to audit the books and verify their accuracy in accordance with generally accepted accounting principles. If a note to the auditor's statement indicates that the firm has not confirmed the accuracy of the data, don't waste your time reading further. If the audit firm confirms the data, you may want to review the remainder of the report.

Whenever a company has a bad year based on actions of the president, chief executive officer, and/or chairman, the report will include a statement like, "Due to international monetary fluctuations and our international investment in XX..., etc." You will not see an admission that, "We fouled up by making some wrong decisions and we'll try to do better next year." Some company executives are honest about errors in judgment and some play the "blame game," taking credit for progress and blaming others for setbacks. (More will be said about company executives in Chapter 14.) You will, however, find accurate accounting data in the financial reports included in an annual report. You can review financial trends related to income, profits, expenses, and much more. Careful reading of an annual report will tell you where a company has been and where it's going.

In case of a privately held company, only the owners and the Internal Revenue Service see the financial data. The owner of a privately held company has no requirement to make financial data public. One exception is that an executive hired by an owner may have access to financial data in order to make prudent business decisions. If a privately held company seeks a loan from a financial institution, the bank or other entity will want to review financial data to judge the risk associated with a loan.

Cost Accounting and Managerial Accounting

Cost accounting determines the costs of manufacturing a product or providing a service. This type of accounting can be very complex. Cost accounting is a division of managerial accounting, the function that provides accurate information to management of the company to enable managers to prepare budgets and review personnel performance.

Managerial accounting includes the costs mentioned previously. It also includes performance reports which are the comparisons of predicted with actual results (sales and profit). Such reports are one type of Variance report. Sales backlogs are also included in managerial accounting reports.

The names of the functions are appropriate. Cost accounting deals with costs of production of goods or services. Managerial accounting involves both cost accounting and information from other company areas, and its reports enable managers to make educated decisions.

Publicly traded companies must also submit certain reports to the U.S. Securities and Exchange Commission (SEC) and comply with certain accounting requirements. A company that issues stocks or bonds to be traded on the market must follow certain procedures in accordance with SEC regulations. While the annual report contains much information of interest to the general public, the SEC requires far more information, including details of the backgrounds of top level managers.

The Sarbanes-Oxley Act of 2002, also known as the Public Company Accounting Reform and Investor Protection Act of 2002, and commonly called SOX or Sarbox, was enacted July 30, 2002. It is a federal law, named after its sponsors, Senator Paul Sarbanes (D-MD) and Representative Michael G. Oxley (R-OH), and enacted in response to a number of major corporate and accounting scandals including those affecting Enron, Tyco International, Adelphia, and WorldCom. The unethical and illegal activities of the CEOs and other high level managers of these companies made them wealthy at the expense of the shareholders. The companies ultimately collapsed and the shareholders lost their investments. Supporters of SOX say that it restored confidence in securities markets by imposing stricter accounting controls; others feel it is overly complex and has not produced the desired results.

It may be helpful to review some of the costs itemized by accounting personnel. The two major categories are *fixed* and *variable*. These and other costs were discussed in Chapter 5 on break-even analysis. Some examples of fixed costs are:

- Depreciation on plant and equipment
- Rentals
- Salaries of research staff
- Salaries of executive staff
- General office expenses

Some examples of direct or variable costs are:

- Factory labor
- Materials
- Sales commissions
- Raw materials used
- Direct labor

Accounting System Procedures

An efficient accounting system tracks every transaction by recording all transactions accurately and honestly in the company's "books." Smaller transactions may be grouped for convenience in a "petty cash" category. Large transactions are recorded separately. The definition of a "large transaction" depends on the size of the company. Generally, a petty cash transaction involves a few dollars; no magic number separates a petty cash transaction from a large transaction. The determination depends on the size of the company and accepted procedures.

The accounting procedures include the bookkeeping process. In this, a series of things is included. Some are:

- Original documents. These are the documents that record the transactions at the time they are made and include receiving records, checks, employee time cards, etc.
- Journals. These are the "books of original entry." The transactions are listed in chronological order in the journals. There is always a general journal. There can be several special journals that contain certain types of transactions. There are sales jour-

nals, purchasing journals, and cash journals, which include respectively, sales, purchases, and cash transactions.

Your original documents may be computer files instead of actual paper. In this case the computer system (hardware and software) should be validated to ensure that no data is changed or lost. As an added precaution there should be limited access—password accessibility—to the financial data to preclude not only unauthorized personnel from seeing the data but also to ensure that no information is changed or deleted accidentally or deliberately.

Ledgers

To make journal information more accessible, entries in journals are individually posted (transferred or entered) to ledger accounts. An account is a record of increases or decreases in assets, liabilities, income, expenses, and capital items. A book containing a number of accounts is called a ledger. Assume you own a small business and make a cash purchase of a certain type of machine used in your production process. (You may not always purchase equipment for cash; we include a cash example for simplicity purposes.) Therefore, you *credit* the asset account (you received the machine) and you *debit* the cash account (you paid for the machine). You "account" for money earned or spent and assets received or used.

Financial Statements

These statements are prepared periodically to provide information to management, the general public, and regulatory agencies. They include the profit and loss statement, balance sheet, and other statements as described in the chapter on finance (Chapter 4).

Conclusions

Now that you know about the accounting function, what are you going to do with the knowledge? First, you must remain aware of the expenses required to run your department. You must also know how the company runs financially and know where your department fits into the scheme.

This leads to budgeting issues. The more effectively you utilize your budget, the larger amount you may get the next time you ask for a budget increase. Let's use an example here. Assume you are walking down a street with your fiancé and you ask your fiancé, with whom you are deeply in love, to hold your hand. Your fiancé replies, "No, thanks." You begin to wonder, if your fiancé loves you, why can't you hold hands while walking along a street. Now extend this analogy to your company.

Your company says it loves you. You ask for money in next year's budget. If other departments have budgets that are significantly larger than yours and you feel you are not getting a fair share, ask yourself whether your company really loves you. The amount of money allocated to your department will not be identical to amounts allotted to other departments; some are larger, some are smaller, and they fill different functions. The magnitude or tightness of your budget is a measure of how much your company loves you. If other departments have ample budgets and yours is unrealistically tight, then your company or your division may not think as highly of your operation as you would like. Consider another possibility. The company may be in dire straits and facing financial problems. If this is so, no department will have an ample budget and all managers have a big job to make the company solvent again. If you are performing well and your company indicates you are performing well, it will give you reasonable funds with which to work because the company knows it takes money to make money.

You don't have to be an accountant, but you should know what the accounting function is and what the difference is between accounting and financial management. And if you manage a department you must function as an accountant and a financial manager to run it properly.

PART II

ELEMENTS OF THE TECHNICAL AREA

10
TECHNICAL FUNCTION
Overview

As we consider many aspects of the technical function, common terms we will use include:

- Technology
- Invention
- Patent
- Innovation
- Research and development

In the scientific world, terms such as *research and development* are tossed around as loosely as the term *marketing* is overused in the business world. Marketing is a "glamour" term. While many people claim to work in marketing, few truly do. A similar dynamic can be observed in technological areas: some people who do not work in research and development say they do and actually do, while others, who don't try to categorize their work, actually focus on research and technological activities.

We will explain the various aspects of research and development. If you are a technical manager, you must clearly understand these aspects to prepare budgets and also determine your return on investment (ROI) resulting from budgeted activities.

Assume that you manufacture T-shirts with various silk-screened designs. You may have one employee in your small business. Suppose you decide that you want to manufacture T-shirts from different fabrics so that they may be more wrinkle-free, water-resistant, or whatever. You obtain samples from your materials supplier and wash them, dry them, and deliberately wrinkle them to see whether they resist wrinkles. This is research.

You might ask the supplier of your coloring materials to provide you with swatches of materials dyed with different colors because you want to see how light-sensitive or fade-resistant the colors are on the fabrics you just researched. You may want to see how the colors withstand washing and drying. This also is research.

After you decide on a new fabric and new colors and you combine them, you are ready to move into the development phase of research and development. If you queried your existing customers regarding what fabrics and colors they may want in the future, you would have performed market research. Major corporations spend millions of dollars a year on research and development functions and employ thousands of people on their research and development staffs. The principle is the same as the one you applied to your T-shirt business; the difference is that large corporations work on a far larger scale. Research and development in a large company may be two separate functions contained in separate buildings or both functions may be handled by a single group.

The development segment of research and development usually includes a product or a process model to determine the feasibility of converting a new idea into a product. In the T-shirt scenario above, you would make a few shirts and test them by having people wear them outdoors in the sunlight, wash them, and wear them again and again until you are convinced that you have a satisfactory product. Automobile manufacturers build cars prior to production, run them on a test track, and measure various parameters to determine whether the new product meets their requirements. The will also measure additional characteristics to ensure that the new parameters do not interfere with or change existing ones. If a car manufacturer installs a GPS system in its cars, it will test the GPS and other functions to be sure that the air conditioning and other systems continue to function effectively.

Basic Research

Basic research formerly involved scientific investigation of a chemical or other item, usually without knowing the ultimate use of the knowledge gained. This is no longer the case. Basic research is still conducted, but practitioners have some knowledge about the potential uses for the information acquired. For example, the nature of light may be investigated without a definite outcome in mind. However, potential uses include communications, energy transfer mechanisms, and other applications. Another example is research to determine DNA sequences of humans. Learning more about which genes control what functions may lead to cures for diseases, although the initial research was intended purely to gain knowledge. Sea life research may lead to applications in the area of food production. The general direction of basic research is known but the end application is not.

One of the best attributes of a researcher is an inquisitive mind. Asking why something happens and then continuing to ask "what if..." is one characteristic of a good researcher. Another is perseverance. If he makes a "discovery," no one knows if he is right or wrong—yet.

Applied Research

Applied research is directed toward particular applications. For example, when a pharmaceutical company directs research toward a compound that will reduce high blood pressure, it has already identified the causes of high blood pressure and directs its research to compounds that will overcome or circumvent these causes. Vasodilator compounds dilate veins and arteries in the circulatory system, thereby reducing blood pressure. Blood vessel dilation is one mechanism used to lower blood pressure. A tranquilizer that calms a person and thereby reduces stress may also lower blood pressure; this represents another route to be studied. Both efforts are examples of applied research: we seek a certain end and direct our research toward achieving that end.

Another area of applied research is fiber optics. This technology produced transmission lines capable of carrying much more data than earlier metal conductor lines. Wireless technology coupled with the digital transmission of data led to enormous strides in communication of information via computer systems, smart phones, high definition television, and other devices. The details of research and development are covered more thoroughly in Chapter 13.

Invention

An invention is a device, technique, or process that will result in a significant change in a technological application. The application is vital to the invention. Although some inventors have devised many new ideas, they had no immediate applications and thus were not true inventions. You must be creative to invent and if you invent something, you must be ready to answer certain questions:

- What is it?
- What does it do?
- Why is it better than what we already have?

If you want to make money from your invention, answer the following questions:

- Can it be made readily?
- Will people buy it?

Many people think an invention must be patented. No invention must be patented. A patent provides legal protection for the inventor of a process or product, so pursuing a patent is a prudent step. Why would you not patent an invention? When an inventor applies for a patent, records filed with the patent office are open for public inspection. While a patent grants exclusivity for 17 years, the process reveals details of your invention to the general public. Some companies such as producers of rubber and plastic items elect not to patent their formulations. They base this practice on the belief that requirements of their production technique (time, temperature, pressure, etc.) cannot be duplicated without knowledge of the formula and other conditions relevant to the process. In essence, they acquire protection for an indefinite time simply by not revealing the formulation and conditions of manufacture. Most companies, however, prefer to patent their products and processes and reap all the rewards they can in their 17 years of exclusivity.

Do not think you will be able to attract investors simply because you invented something that you think is great. Prudent investors—those who survive in the financial world are prudent—invest money only if you are willing to invest some of your own. Being an inventor is usually not sufficient to convince investors to provide money to you or your company. You must be willing to invest your own money too.

A large company might buy or license your patent. If a large company agrees to talk to you, you will have to produce the patent along with a model or results obtained from a model. However, large companies usually don't want to talk to new inventors for two reasons:

1. The "not invented here" (NIH) syndrome. You may think that an executive of a major company would welcome you and your invention because you can help his company make a new product. That seldom occurs. Large companies don't want to have to admit that an "outsider" invented items they produce. This has nothing to do with the quality of your invention; it relates to human frailties and insecurities.

2. Large companies don't want to be involved in lawsuits. Companies have been sued by inventors in cases where the companies were working on products or processes at the same time individuals approached them with patented inventions. When the products reached the market, the inventors sued. In such cases, the company would win by proving it had the technology and did not steal the concept. However, large companies do not want the expense, aggravation, and bad publicity arising from such suits and therefore prefer not to entertain ideas from independent inventors.

If you are an inventor, think carefully about who will buy or license your patent or product and how you will approach such a buyer. Library research is in order. Think of one company that may be interested, find its SIC or NAICS designation, and research other companies that have that SIC or NAICS (as explained in Chapter 3). Contact the company via letter with a follow-up phone call, or engage a sales and marketing firm to make the contact.

If you decide to start a company and produce your product, innovation centers that may or may not be associated with your local economic development authority can assist you. Many of these centers are at major universities.

The general characteristics of an inventor include (1) extreme curiosity, (2) determination, (3) persistence to an extreme level, (4) positive thinking, and (5) creativity—a quality that is difficult to define. Creativity may be the ability to relate facts that most other people cannot relate and put them together in such a way that they lead to a conclusion that ultimately results in a new idea or invention.

Patents

As we mentioned earlier, while an inventor is not required to obtain a patent, doing so is usually a good idea. When a person invents a product or process in the course of his work for a major corporation, the patent is assigned to the corporation. The inventor's name is on the patent but the patent is *assigned* to the corporation. If the person has earned elite status in the hierarchy of inventors within a company, he or she may be in a position to share in the monetary rewards (via profit sharing or on a percentage basis). This is rarely the case for two reasons. First, many inventions do not result from the efforts of one single inventor; they come from integrated efforts of a number of people in a company. Second, the corporation is far larger than any inventor and it will prevail.

Someone may tell you that you don't need an attorney; you can perform a patent search, apply for a patent for only $300, and save yourself a lot of money. Yes, you can do the required search and prepare the documents but it will cost far more than $300. Typically, the costs to pursue a patent are:

Search	$500 to $1,000
Patent application	$2,800 to $10,000
Government filing fee	$340
Required drawings	$250 to $500

If you perform a patent search and prepare your own patent application, you can save the money required for the first two items. However, government patent examiners frequently "bounce" applications back to applicants and patent attorneys know how to resubmit them and ultimately get patents issued. If you can handle a resubmission, you can probably prepare your own application. The filing fee goes to the U.S. Patent Office.* Most attorneys will treat the filing fee as a client cost and bill you for the amount. You may wish to browse the Patent Office website to examine other patents and get familiar with submission requirements.

---

* The official name is the United States Patent and Trademark Office; its website is www.USPTO.gov.

As to friends who suggest you file your own patent, ask how many patents they obtained by pursuing the process on their own. If they have performed their own searches and filings and are wealthy, listen. If not, ask whether they would drill and fill their own teeth to avoid paying a dentist.

Think carefully about filing for a patent. The figures cited above are subject to change and the process is complex. Consider the cost of obtaining a patent relative to your anticipated income from the invention. Now you have the proper perspective. If your invention is only going to earn $1,000 or $2,000 for you, your market is very small and the need for patenting is questionable except for the personal satisfaction of having a patent issued in your name.

The figures above do not represent idle speculation. They cover the common range of costs. My two patents are on an environmentally friendly, sustained release, chemical delivery product. The patent applications were submitted through my patent attorney, Eric La Morte, of Yardley, Pennsylvania. He is one of the 1% of attorneys registered with the Patent Office (one requirement is an undergraduate degree in a science or engineering field), and his services have been worth every dollar I have spent. For further reading on patents and marketing ideas, I recommend *Millions from the Mind,* 2nd Edition (Alan R. Tripp, Taletyano Press, 2003). I read this book, spoke with Alan, and strongly suggest that anyone interested in patents, and particularly those who choose to pursue a patent independently, read it.

Innovation

An innovation is really the application of an invention or an idea. It can be small or large, depending on whether it represents a major breakthrough or an improvement to an existing product or process. What seem to be major innovations sometimes result from a series of smaller innovations. For example, after the telephone was invented, digital transformation and transportation of information and other innovations led to the modern fax machine. No one decided 80 years ago to invent a fax machine.* The point is that while innovations are significant in their own right, they also lead to other innovations. The

---

* The fax machine got its name from the word "facsimile."

more knowledge we have, the more we can accomplish by building upon it.

Technology

Today, we link science and technology through many science-based technological developments. However, technology did not always connect with science. In the agricultural societies of the 18th century, changing the shape of a tool—an innovation so to speak—was considered new technology. Certainly, the modifications of farming tools to be pulled by animals constituted a new technology. In more recent times, the mechanization of hand tools into earth movers and tractors led to further technologies.

Now, linking technology with science, for example, in digital electronics devices, is common practice. Other science-based industries are based on chemistry, physics, molecular biology, and mathematics. The computer is probably the most prominent technological development of our time.

The basketballs used by the National Basketball Association (NBA) were formerly made from leather. Modern basketballs are composed of composites of various materials specifically designed to produce the same bounce, exhibit much more durability, and last much longer. Modern technology, by virtue of computers, new composite materials, electronics, chemistry, physics, and more, plays a major role in all aspects of life. We can no longer lock ourselves into a particular definition of technology. We all have opportunities to advance it. If you have an idea as a result of asking yourself the "what if…?" question, refine your idea by thinking about it in more detail and then pursue its application. You may provide great benefit to yourself and to society.

11
QUALITY CONTROL

Quality control and quality assurance are different. The difference may be slight or great, depending on the company, its products, philosophies, and size. We briefly discussed the importance of quality in Chapter 8 and will cover it in more detail in this chapter.

Generally speaking, quality assurance encompasses the overall quality function and includes quality control. The quality assurance department determines which product attributes are required to satisfy customers and sets up specifications that products must meet to *assure quality.*

Quality control involves sampling input raw materials, work in progress, and the final product. This group conducts tests to determine whether the product will provide the quality that customers expect.

In small companies employing 10 to 20 persons, a single individual (possibly a staff engineer or chemist) may handle more than one function, including quality assurance and quality control. Companies with 100 to 200 employees may have a dedicated quality assurance department that will handle the quality control function. In large operations, quality assurance and quality control people are prohibited from participating in production—manufacturing persons are not allowed to police themselves. These companies usually operate with separate quality assurance and quality control functions.

Within a company, different types of products may require separate quality control and quality assurance speciaists. For example, a company that makes pharmaceuticals as tablets and injected compounds may operate two distinct quality areas that report to a director. While all the company's products are subject to FDA regulations, the manufacturing processes for these products differ. Thus conventional tablet manufacture and sterile production specialists would oversee quality in their respective areas and report to the director of quality.

In this chapter, we will assume that the company has already determined the quality attributes required to satisfy customers. We will discuss the quality control function as it measures and/or controls quality.

Consumer Quality Issues

Consumers determine satisfactory quality levels. For instance, what determines the quality of a suit? A combination of fabric, quality of construction, fit, appearance, and other factors. Generally, materials and workmanship exhibited in the finished product seem to determine quality for consumers. One person may be content with a $200 suit and another may purchase a $1,000 suit. Is the $1,000 suit five times as good as the $200 suit? The person who can spend $1,000 for a suit thinks so—even if the materials and workmanship of the more expensive suit do not justify the price difference. Is a $280,000 Rolls Royce twenty times as valuable as a $14,000 Toyota? It is to the Rolls Royce owner; otherwise he would not have purchased it. You can buy an accurate watch for $100. Why would you spend $5000 on a Rolex? If your income is at the level of a typical Rolex buyer's income, you may feel a $5,000 watch is worth the price.

Quality in large part depends on customers, what they expect of the product, and more specifically, what they expect of the product attributes that constitute overall product performance.

Produce the Best!

No one would argue with the statement that a company should make the best product it can. However, that aspiration is not always practical. While Part 2 of this book deals with technical issues, technical operations are closely connected to other business areas. For example, technical areas have the responsibility of satisfying customers after marketing determines customer needs. If your company has determined that customers who fit the demographic profile to which your company is selling require a certain quality level, *your product* should be directed to that quality level. Achieving a higher quality level will cost more and could eventually price your product out of your desired market segment. If you market cars in the under-$14,000 price range (your chosen market segment), you are not going to test every engine to ensure that it will run for 300,000 miles; your customers will not expect to drive their cars 300,000 miles. Mercedes Benz owners expect 300,000 miles of performance and the company designs and tests its products accordingly to satisfy customers in its market segment.

The quality level sought by your customers should be known *before* your product goes into mass production. Quality requirements may have to be adjusted somewhat if they either cannot be met or are met too easily.

Quality Characteristics

Tests to determine quality levels are designed to measure certain characteristics: (1) level of quality and (2) consistency in meeting the required level of quality.

Chapter 6 discussed statistics and normal (also called Gaussian or bell-shaped) distribution. Assume you are a manufacturer of 28-ounce bottles of juice. Each bottle has a "head space" to allow expansion and overfill. You want to fill each bottle with exactly 28 ounces. Figure 11.1 reveals that the average fill is 28 ounces with a narrow distribution about that average—that is, a few bottles contain more and a few contain less. This distribution indicates that you are achieving the 28-ounce fill requirement.

Figure 11.2 confirms the average fill of 28 ounces with an equal number of overfills and underfills, but the range is much wider. Overfills are far above the desired 28 ounces and underfills are far

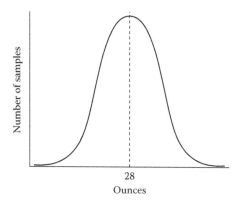

Figure 11.1 Gaussian distribution.

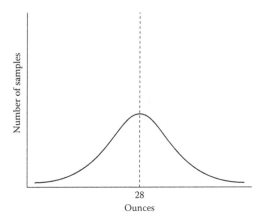

Figure 11.2 Wide Gaussian distribution.

under the requirement. This means your system should be "tightened up." Figure 11.3 shows a distribution skewed to the left. This indicates the system is running well but producing many underfills—an undesirable narrow distribution about a low value. The production line equipment should be adjusted to uniformly attain the desired 28-ounce fill.

Another way of presenting data is illustrated in Figure 11.4. The horizontal axis reflects the number of samples or production items and the vertical axis indicates test result values (ounces of liquid in bottles). The desired (target) value is represented by a horizontal line drawn at that level and labeled as such. The line above it represents the upper control limit (UCL) and the line below it indicates the lower

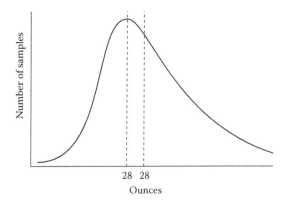

Figure 11.3 Skewed distribution.

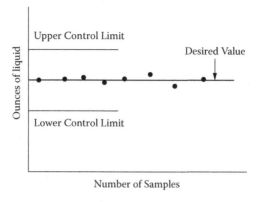

Figure 11.4

control limit (LCL). Sample values are plotted on this chart and produce a scatter diagram depicting the performance of your system.

We have learned how to determine accuracy and consistency by
applying numerical values to manufacturing performance. We performed similar operations in Chapter 6. *Keep in mind that any system
requires analysis of both accuracy and consistency of the degree of accuracy,*
whether defined by numbers or via another method.

You may want to measure other attributes of your product, such as
the acidity, clarity, or color of the juice in the above example. Select
the measurements that most effectively provide the quality information you need.

Total Quality Management (TQM)

We discussed TQM in Chapter 8—the dedication of an entire organization to producing quality for consumers and those in the "production line."* Instead of simply "sorting out the bad ones" at the end of
a production line, TQM minimizes the number of inferior products.
In theory, the goal is to produce no inferior products. If you practice
this principle in your job and in all other phases of your life, you can
have a very rewarding life.

---

* "Production line" in this context means every person from the CEO to shipping
  dock employees.

Malcolm Baldrige Award

The federal government honors a few companies annually with the Malcolm Baldrige Award for excellence in quality assurance and quality control. Malcolm Baldrige was the 26th Secretary of Commerce, nominated by President Ronald Reagan in 1980 and confirmed by the Senate in 1981. He accomplished much during his tenure as Secretary and was considered an excellent manager and also a colorful personality (he was an avid horseman and earned several awards on the rodeo circuit). Baldrige died in July 1987 as a result of a rodeo accident. Thereafter the Reagan administration initiated the Malcolm Baldrige Award to honor companies that show dedication to quality. Names of winners and other information can be found on the National Institute of Standards and Technology website www.nist.gov.

Quality Levels and Costs: Different Views

Some companies believe that they can achieve extremely high quality levels and also reduce costs, i.e., the highest quality actually costs a manufacturer less. The theory here is that correct performance at every step in the production process will minimize the need for extensive inspection at the end. Only a rapid inspection by employees or robots will be required. The principle is correct: it's easier and less costly to do a job right in the first place than to do it wrong and redo it.

We hear a lot about Six Sigma (6 σ) quality. What is it and how is it attained? In Chapter 6, we showed that a 3 σ quality level indicated that 99.7% (actually 99.73%) of all the parts produced were made correctly. That means 997,300 parts of every 1,000,000 produced will be satisfactory and 2,700 will be defective. The 99.7% does not sound so good when viewed that way. Achieving 6 σ quality means producing 3.4 defective parts *per million*; 999,996 parts out of a million meet the desired quality level.

A September 7, 1992 *Newsweek* article titled "The Cost of Quality," by Jay Mathews and Peter Ketel stated that, "Faced with hard times, business sours on 'total quality management'." The authors cited an example of a company so obsessed with improving its inventory process that it spent a fortune on a state-of-the-art computer system; as a result the wholesale cost of producing a 25-cent item "soared to a ridiculous $2.89." They mentioned that (in 1992) the cost of quality was questionable.

These opposing views represent an interesting polarity. What do you do? Look at your product, your company, your philosophy, your customers, and the costs of your quality level. This book cannot tell you what quality level to achieve. Only you can determine that. It does, however, equip you with factors to consider when determining quality level for your products.

Customer Service

Service to customers usually extends beyond the purchase. Anyone who has purchased a modern electronic product, such as a smart phone, knows that the reality is far more complicated. You purchase an item advertised as "user friendly" and assume it will be easy to operate. The set-up required to enable the device to function is challenging and the 400 page manual is cumbersome. You call the customer service number and learn that all representatives are busy.... After a long wait, someone answers; you explain the problem; you're referred to another department. You may be transferred (and face another wait while you "hold") or must hang up and call another number. When the second person refers you back to the first, you realize you are in an endless loop. You may have purchased a quality item, but it's useless without genuine customer service. The difficulty of using the product and lack of customer service indicate your purchase is not a quality product.

Antivirus programs for computers serve as another example of this dynamic. After you buy one and install it, it blocks far more than viruses; it blocks the programs you need. You want to contact customer service to resolve the problem and learn the only way to contact the company is when you receive a service renewal notice. Learn what not to do from these examples. When you design a product, ensure quality from design through production and provide after-sale service.

When you buy a large ticket item like a car, ask the salesperson for the customer service phone number. In the presence of the salesperson, call the number (if you're put on hold before the purchase, imagine the treatment you will get after you buy the product). As you call, note the salesperson's facial expression. It may indicate fear of losing a sale or it may change to a confident smile. The salesperson knows the level of customer service you can expect. This type of call can make your decision easy.

12

TECHNICAL SERVICE

The meaning of "technical service" differs among companies and industries. In essence, technical service is what a company wants it to be; it may even serve as a catch-all for activities that don't fit into other categories.

Ask yourself now:

- What is technical service in your company?
- What do you want it to be?
- What is the difference between your customer service and your technical service?

Definition

The technical service function (person, department, division, etc.) serves others within and possibly outside the organization with regard to technical aspects of the product or process by which the product is made. Customer service normally handles nontechnical or minimally technical aspects of consumer products. The names clearly indicate the functions.

To whom does the technical service function respond? Figure 12.1 indicates that technical service can be external or internal. If external, it is usually set up to serve customers or potential customers. Internal technical service handles in-house issues for other areas such as research and development, legal, sales, and others.

Why is it important to define service parameters? If you do not clearly define the scope and responsibilities of your technical service area, everyone in the company will call technical service with questions. As a result, the department will be overloaded with work, very little of which will make a better product or produce more sales. Figure 12.1 shows departments that may use technical service, but technical service can also perform preventive functions, investigate

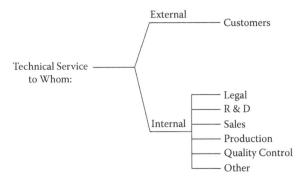

Figure 12.1 Technical service—external and internal.

potential problems with a product or process, and correct them. In some cases, a very narrow line separates technical service activity from research and development.

If your technical service group will respond to in-house customers (Figure 12.1), it must be ready to respond rapidly. Technical problems impose urgency. A backlog of technical problems usually means a lack of capable people available to solve problems fast. This lack will cost money; it is expensive to engage qualified technical problem solvers on short notice.

Why should you define whether technical service will work to prevent problems or respond to customer problems? Speed is of the essence in responding to customer problems. Preventive work usually allows more planning. This difference affects the department set-up and work schedules (see Figure 12.2).

Think also about contacts with external and internal (Figure 12.1) customers. Can a technical service representative speak and correspond with someone outside the firm without having a salesperson present? Policies and practices vary among companies and products. Many salespeople want to be involved in any discussions with their

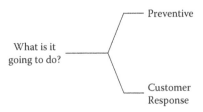

Figure 12.2

customers. Will a technical serviceperson travel with a salesperson to the facility of a customer to identify a problem? Some policy should be established to cover the interactions of sales and technical people with customers and potential customers. The best answer would appear to have a salesperson and technical person function as a team. That way, the salesperson won't err on technical matters and the technical person will not cross the line into sales.

To whom should the head of technical service report? Should he or she report to the vice president of operations or the vice president of technology? Before you can answer that you must consider an equipment issue. If your technical service staff requires expensive equipment like mass spectrometers, you must determine whether your research and development area has such equipment, and decide whether technical service will use it. If the research and development department in the technology area purchased the equipment and the technical service group in the operations area uses it, the vice president of technology may not want R & D equipment used by operations people.

If both groups use the same equipment, you must determine whether it is reasonable to buy a second set or have the two areas share it. Before you purchase equipment, determine who will use it, who will pay for it, and what types of work it will handle. An alternative is for technical service to rent expensive equipment from R & D via an accounting transfer of budget funds. After these issues are resolved, you can decide to whom the technical service group will report.

In most cases a technical service representative (tech rep) can solve problems in person or by phone. Many companies outsource this function to third parties, either domestically or foreign. Outsourcing is discussed in more detail in Chapter 17. The term "offshore" is used instead of "foreign." Maybe they think it sounds less distant. In these cases the representatives are taught rather good English by the third party contractor. They usually answer the phone promptly and solve the problem during the conversation.

Summary

This chapter cannot determine an ideal solution for your company. You must determine the best set-up for technical service based on your product and your customers. However, it is wise to consider certain questions:

- What is the nature of the product?
- What is the nature of problems to which technical service will respond?
- Are the "customers" of technical service internal or external?
- How much time will be available to respond to internal or external customers and handle preventive functions? (Keep in mind that the department and/or employees can serve dual functions.)
- What equipment is required?
- Will technical service have its own equipment or share equipment assigned to another department?
- To whom will the technical service department report?

Consideration of the above factors will assist you immensely in determining the size, organization, and work assignments of a technical service group that will make the service more satisfactory to your customers and to you.

13

RESEARCH AND DEVELOPMENT

Overview

Chapter 10 briefly introduced the research and development function. In this chapter we will address issues such as:

- What is research and development?
- Why is it needed? (If, in fact, you believe it is needed.)
- How does the research and development function relate to the rest of a company?
- What is your laboratory structure?
- How do your research and development and technical services differ?
- How will you direct research and development?
- What is your company's chain of command for research and development?

It may be helpful to define research and development separately. Simply put, research is exploring new ideas. Development can be considered a phase of research or the next step beyond research. Table 13.1 details various aspects of research and development. As a project advances from basic research to production, the probabilities associated with it increase significantly. Basic research does not always have an end result. More predictability surrounds applied research, and predictability continues to increase as an idea approaches the production stage that will generate money.

A review of Table 13.1 will show that as we increase from basic research to production, the probabilities associated with what we are going to learn increase significantly. We are not sure what we are going to get out of basic research. Then we have more predictability associated with applied research, and then more as we go down the

Table 13.1   Research Classifications

TYPE OF CLASSIFICATION	WHAT IT IS	OUTPUT
Basic research	A scientific investigation of some phenomenon without a definite realization of what practical application will come from it	Knowledge
Applied research	An investigation into knowledge, new or old, that already exists, in an effort to find particular applications of that knowledge	Knowledge directly related to specific applications
Development	Further exploration and testing of a potential application to determine the feasibility of a new product or process	A product model or process system model and the feasibility and/or probability associated with it
Pilot Plant	The testing of a product or process using the specifications that emerged from the development stage	Economic feasibility, i.e., the costs likely to be associated with this product or process when in production
Initial production	The designing and implementation of production equipment for this new process or product with the testing and adaptation until satisfactory running of the system is attained… or the decision is made to cease the system	The complete operational system

chart. Another thing also changes. The probability of money coming into the firm increases more as the project gets closer to the production stage. Most companies want to get to this stage (the stage of making money) as soon as possible.

Table 13.1 shows the various classifications of research and even includes initial production under the heading of research. As you review this table, you may choose other words to describe what occurs within your company, but this chart should give you a good overview of the types of research and why, here, we are considering development as a stage of research.

Some companies do not conduct their own research. They contract it out to research organizations. Figure 13.1 indicates that industry, the federal government, and academia conduct a large variety of research projects. Industry investigates relevant products and processes. Small

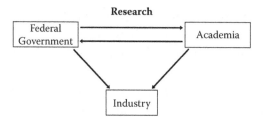

Figure 13.1

companies with strong research capabilities have been purchased and became divisions of larger companies. In fact, some companies are founded with the plan to be purchased by a larger company. Many agencies of the federal government perform research applicable to their operations, and much of the information is available to the general public. Information about various agencies, their responsibilities, and how to contact them can be found at http://www.usa.gov/Agencies/Federal/All_Agencies/index.shtml.

Academic institutions are excellent sources of research. If you require research in a particular area, approach a university with a relevant program (e.g., an agricultural college would be helpful if you sell food products) and meet professors who supervise graduate students who conduct research. In many cases, a grant from your company will make information resulting from research projects available to your company before general publication. I am not advocating industry control of research projects of graduate students. However, it is an intelligent way of obtaining the information you seek. Your company, the college, and the graduate student all benefit. Figure 13.1 indicates a number of options available for obtaining research information. An aspect to consider, however, is that you relinquish a measure of control when you contract a research project to an outside organization.

Benefits of Research and Development

Research and development functions keep a company aware of new developments and future possibilities. Research and development activities yield results that cure illnesses, save lives, provide a high quality of life, generally make work easier and life more pleasurable. Another valid reason is simply to satisfy our curiosity about things.

If your company manufactures golf tees or clothespins you may justifiably question the need for extensive research, but improvements are possible even in industries that appear not to depend on research breakthroughs.

If you made manual typewriters and chose not to advance to electric, electronic, and computer word processing capabilities, you would probably not have a market anywhere in the world.

Around 1967 and 1968, 90% of all watches were manufactured in Switzerland, and then in 1968, the digital watch was invented. People now could see the actual digits that would indicate the time of day. Initially, you had to push the little button in order to get the watch to light up. Subsequently, the watches have improved over the last 40 years and now you just look at them and time is displayed along with various other information, and much more information can be presented at the touch of a button. The Swiss watchmakers believed that people would not want to change and would prefer the former style—the way watches have always shown the time—and hence, did not immediately go into the digital watch and thereby lost a significant share of the market. On the other hand, various companies in the United States started manufacturing digital watches. The digital watch became commonplace. By the way, where do you think the digital watch was invented? If you haven't guessed, it was invented in Switzerland. The market has swung back to the "regular, analog" watches, but for a long time digital watches were very popular.

Here's another case. One company had the research and development capability to find a new use for a rejected product. In the early 1970s, Upjohn discovered that its minoxidil prescription drug used to reduce hypertension caused excessive growth of hair. Looking at this side effect from a new view, Upjohn scientists investigated its efficacy for hair growth. In 1988, the product (renamed Rogaine) was put on the market as a pharmaceutical formulation to aid hair growth. Rogaine sales total about a quarter of a billion dollars annually.

A new technology now in common use is the global positioning system (GPS) that can pinpoint a location to within 30 feet. Initially used by the military and civilian aviation, it is now available for use in automobiles. Hikers use hand held GPS units to navigate.

Things seemingly as simple as cell phones (which are not really that simple) that do so many things including taking pictures and recording voices are the result of R & D. The ability of police departments to trace the specific towers that conveyed cell phone calls is the result of R & D. Making automobiles more fuel efficient and also making automobiles that run on other than oil based fuels are research efforts that benefit us. Gene splicing specifically, and biotechnology more generally, continue to lead to more productive food harvests and to new pharmaceuticals. These are a few examples of how research has helped us. It costs a lot of money to conduct research and more to take the results through development, but the rewards can be great.

Whether a company needs research and development, and the degree to which these functions are needed, depend on the company and its philosophies, as determined by the board of directors, the CEO, and other executives.

R & D and Its Relationships with Other Areas of the Company

Where do research and development functions fit within a company? In Chapter 1 we compared a business to a mobile and showed how each area connected to other areas and how any major change necessitated a shift of the others to regain equilibrium. A business continually tries to displace the equilibrium by moving forward; as one area changes, the others must change to accommodate it.

When research and development efforts design or improve a product or process, the areas of sales, marketing, manufacturing, and others must adapt to regain equilibrium. Let's take a case where research and development improves an existing process to save time and money. By using a more expensive material, the company can increase production. The increase in product made per hour far offsets the cost of the new material, leading to increased profit. Assuming the company makes other products, it may choose to sell more of the item produced via the new process because it can increase production without a major capital expenditure. (It already paid for the research and development.) Sales and marketing must now be prepared to sell more.

No division, department, or area stands alone. If it did, it would constitute a separate company, and might be counterproductive to the corporate goals. The essence of a business is for all of the parts to work together. Management's role is to achieve that symbiosis.

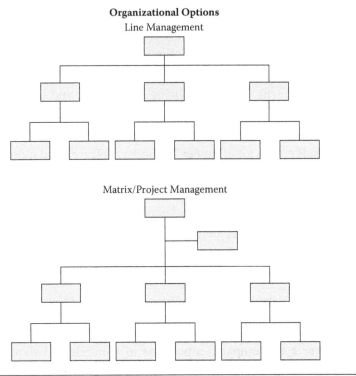

Figure 13.2 Comparison of line management and matrix/project management.

Laboratory Structure

A small company may not need a laboratory. A medium-sized company may have a single laboratory that handles research and development, technical service functions, and quality control. As a company expands, the functions of quality control, technical service, and research and development become more distinct. We have chosen in this book to treat them as separate entities, as is the case in large companies. The size of a company, the philosophies of management, and the nature of its products determine whether research and development will or will not be a separate function.

The two primary organization types common in laboratories are line management and matrix or project management, both of which are shown in Figure 13.2. The line management option is shown in more detail in Figure 13.3, and Figure 13.4 illustrates matrix or project management.

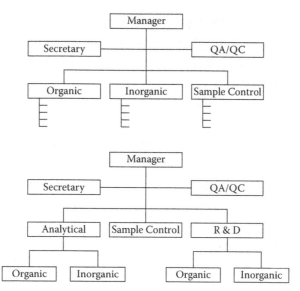

Characteristics:

- Clear line of command
- Responsibility for production well defined
- Works well for production type work

- Provides close supervision
- Working directly for person most influential

Figure 13.3 Line management.

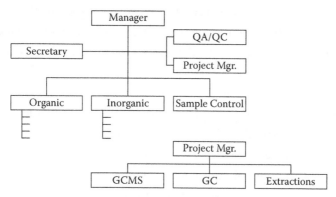

Characteristics:

- Most sensitive to customer's needs
- Select individuals used
- Clear responsibility for the job
- Best for research type activity
- Less direct supervision
- Project members have two bosses

Figure 13.4 Matrix/project management.

Observations of the figures show that for line management there is a clear line of command. This is best for a production type situation. Looking at the project management outline, we see that it is the best for research type activity. It also has the least direct supervision, a characteristic which is good for a research function. Research people do not like to be supervised too directly. However, we see that the project members have two bosses: the laboratory manager and the project manager. Another way of looking at this, and it is a way that exists in many places, is that the project manager may be a highly skilled research person who is directing the various laboratory people involved in a particular project. But the laboratory people really report directly to the laboratory manager, who is the person who is responsible for their evaluations and their raises and all those good things. Where do you think their dedication is going to be? The project management option looks like it works very well, and it can work very well, provided the sensitivities are taken into account first hand.

As with any job in any organization, a person needs to know who his/her boss is. Any person wants to know, and has a right to know, whose input will be considered—and of course by whom that input will be considered—in their next evaluation for promotion and/or salary increase. People always have as their priority the work assigned to them by the person who controls their salary, regardless of whatever other tasks and responsibilities fall their way. Whatever system you select, make sure that everyone knows the hierarchy. For efficiency and for ethics reasons don't let them think person A is evaluating them while person B is actually doing the evaluating. To put it more bluntly, "their first loyalty is to the person who pays them" and they should know who that person is.

The most efficient practice is to provide every person in a laboratory with an entire range of equipment, but that is idealistic and usually not affordable. Therefore, you will devise another arrangement. Some highly complex instruments such as a mass spectrometer require a specialist to run it. Mass spectrometers frequently serve as research instruments and fill another role by processing samples submitted by other areas. Which system—the line, matrix, or a combination—is best for you? Only you can decide based on available equipment, features, advantages and disadvantages, and costs.

Comparison of Research and Development and Technical Service

Research and development and technical service are different functions as noted earlier. Both functions may be handled by a single individual or small group in a small firm. In this case, management may want to keep track of the research and development projects separately from technical service projects for financial purposes, and calculate returns on investment from each function. This is very important in a small growing company in which management may want to expand one function only. If the research and development projects have generated more return on investment (ROI) based on new or improved products or processes than the technical service unit, management may wish to invest more money into research and development to earn more money in the long run.

In a large company, the two functions are distinct and have separate staffs. Chapter 12 discussed the technical service function. This chapter focuses on the research and development function, and by now the difference should be clear. Generally, technical service handles troubleshooting for existing products or processes and "preventive" activities. The research and development function develops new products and processes or attempts to improve existing ones even when there is no problem.

Directing Research and Development Operations

Directing the research and development function of a company requires effective people skills. Much more will be said about people skills in Chapter 16. Research and development people are a "different breed." A good research and development person, department, or division (for the sake of discussion, let's use "department") can produce innovations that generate huge income. It is paradoxical that productivity is sometimes difficult to measure. Of course, in any applied research activity, the goal is defined before work starts, but the R & D success is not measured; it is estimated. Compare this to the sales function whose performance is measurable by comparing current sales to the previous year's sales.

You may point out that all sales of a certain new product resulted from its invention by a research and development department.

Research and development will agree; the sales department may not agree and will assert that sales skill was a contributing factor. This indicates the difficulty of measuring the productivity of a research and development function.

It is appropriate now to cover productivity measurement. Generally, productivity is based on attainment of goals. The manager's responsibility is to direct his department toward meeting those goals.

How do you measure the productivity of a research and development department? Certain parameters can be measured:

- The number of projects completed in a specific period.

    While this is not a measure of productivity, it reveals information about the functioning of the department. The time spent on a project measured as persons/day may be very small; i.e., a company may pursue a lot of small projects at one time. This does not mean the projects are not productive. On the other hand, we cannot claim that a project was more productive because it required more time. The nature of the business determines the number of projects.

- The number of projects carried at a particular point in time.

    This has a similar answer; project activity depends on the nature of the business and the complexity of products or processes involved. No direct correlation exists between the number of projects carried at any one time and department productivity. Researchers must sometimes wait for results of an interim evaluation of a project. This is not a delay; the necessary wait time should be incorporated into a project schedule and staff can work on other projects in the interim. For this reason, the number of projects at a given time is not an indication of productivity.

- Sales generated by research and development efforts.

    If contributions of other departments such as sales, marketing, and manufacturing were not involved, you could consider income from inventions or new processes as a measure of the success or productivity of R & D. The result would not be a dollar-for-dollar comparison of new product sales but it would provide a basis for a project-to-project comparison. Keep in mind the time lag from invention to income flow. An even more complex issue is measuring the productivity of a project aimed at improving a process. This involves measuring the increased efficiency of the improved process.

- Research and development director's monthly report.

    This is the least reliable and is a miniature version of an annual report intended for in-house use. It provides executives and others with information about the progress and status of various projects. It should not lead to the demise of the career of the director who wrote it. Whether the results described were good or not good, it's always advisable to detail the next steps planned for current projects. This tells readers where you plan to go and is always a positive sign.

The point of this section is that you cannot measure the productivity of a research and development department as precisely as you can measure sales or manufacturing performance. Sales figures are tracked consistently. Manufacturing efficiency is measured by comparing inventory produced to inventory returned. While scientists like to be precise, non-quantitative terms (mediocre, good, very good, excellent) may be the only way to describe results. Research and development people rely on faith and their track records. However, better measures are required.

The preferred method is to break a project into phases or steps, define the results desired for the individual steps, and compare the results of each phase to the projected or desired results through the end of the project. Financial implications of research are important but a researcher's primary need is to know how to plan a project and measure successes along the road to completion.

If you direct a research and development function, it is imperative to give researchers a high degree of freedom. Remember the characteristics of a research person? He or she is a positive thinker, a daydreamer, and an explorer who requires freedom. How do you manage this type of person? You provide an atmosphere that is conducive to positive thinking, daydreaming, exploring, and freedom, within certain limits, of course. The main point is that research and development personnel require more freedom and less direction than production line employees. Research and development scientists should be given more freedom than quality control personnel. Quality control people are expected to follow certain procedures and occasionally modify them as required. Research and development people require the freedom to rethink and modify all the time.

Does this mean that you give a scientist a complete laboratory with an unlimited budget, deposit his paychecks, and talk to him at review time? No, it means that you listen to what staff members say, direct them at times, perhaps more subtly or more firmly if they wander off course from the goals of the company or department.

Directing a research and development operation is in large part a guiding and coaching type of managing.

You may wonder whether granting a great deal of freedom to a research and development scientist will lead to projects outside defined parameters or a lack of communication. These unexpected results are unlikely because research people like to talk about their discoveries. We all want recognition and researchers are no exceptions. This does not mean you should sit back and wait until a staff member comes to you to report a discovery. Giving your staff freedom does not mean relinquishing control. Conduct periodic meetings, disseminate data relevant to priorities, and seek information from your research staff. If you keep the reins loose and attract genuine research and development people, you will have a productive department.

PART III

INTEGRATING BUSINESS AND TECHNICAL AREAS FOR PROFIT

14

THE CORPORATION AS A UNIT

An Overview

In Chapter 1, we discussed business in general and talked about various forms: corporation, partnership, and sole proprietorship. This chapter focuses on the functioning of a corporation as a unit. The principles presented apply to partnerships and sole proprietorships as well. The subjects that will be covered include:

- Corporation structure
- Defining your business
- Goal setting and strategic planning
- Management styles

Corporation Structure

A company consists of various departments; we studied a number of them earlier. The departments co-exist and interact (as we shall see to a greater degree in Chapter 15). Individuals' lives consist of various aspects: mental, spiritual, and physical. All these aspects combine within a single individual, similar to the way departments interact within a company. Individuals behave in accordance with how they regard themselves and others. A company's behavior is influenced by the product it wants to sell to customers and the philosophy of its management.

Refer to Figure 14.1. The group at the center, the board of directors, chief executive officer (CEO), and president control the company. They define the direction the company will travel with regard to products and to markets. As the view widens, the pie wedges rep-

Figure 14.1   Corporation structure.

resent areas, departments, or divisions of the company.* Surrounding the company structure are the shareholders who are part owners of the company. Remember, preferred and common stocks are the primary types of stock. The shareholders own the company. They select the board of directors and the board hires the CEO who in turn hires the president.

The outer layer of the circumference of the circle represents stakeholders—people, groups, or agencies with which the company interfaces. Stakeholders do not own the company but have a "stake" in its activities. For example, neighbors of the manufacturing plant are stakeholders in the sense that they do not want their air polluted or their water supply harmed. The bank from which the company borrows money is a stakeholder. Other area banks are stakeholders in the respect that they want to acquire the company's banking business. Local, state, and federal governments are stakeholders in the sense that they enact and enforce regulations that affect the company. Customers are clearly stakeholders. Employees are stakeholders who

---

* The pie wedges represent divisions common to small and large operations. For example, management information service (MIS) was not included because of lack of space.

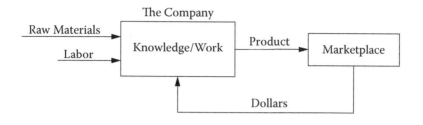

Figure 14.2   Corporate inputs and outputs.

may or may not also be shareholders. They are stakeholders because they produce the company's output and are paid for their efforts. They are responsible to the company and it has a responsibility to them.

Figure 14.2 provides another view. The company combines inputs of raw materials and labor with knowledge and work and produces outputs: products. In the market, products are exchanged for dollars received by the company. We know from Chapter 4 (our discussion of finance) that receipts from sales are used by the company to pay the costs of raw materials, labor, interest on bonds or loans, and taxes; the remainder is profit that is distributed to shareholders (as owners) in the form of dividends or is reinvested to purchase new equipment, build facilities, or launch other projects.

Although shareholders are the true owners, the board of directors and executive staff run the company. We will now discuss the responsibilities of these top level executives.

Chairman of the Board

The chairman of the board of directors "runs the show." The board directs the activities of the company for and in response to shareholders' wishes. The chairman heads the board. Traditionally, the chairman was an employee, usually a president who moved up. In recent years board chairmen are commonly not employees. This is why "cleaning house" sometimes occurs when a new chairman takes over. Having an outside chairman prevents the "good old buddy" situations that in the past developed between the chairman and executives and negatively impacted their companies.

Chief Executive Officer (CEO)

The CEO reports to the chairman; the president and chief operating officer report to the CEO. In effect, the CEO runs the company on a day-to-day basis. The chairman of the board determines the direction and the CEO manages the entire company.

Chief Operating Officer (COO)

The COO is in charge of the operating (manufacturing) divisions of the company. The COO is not responsible for the accounting, legal, or human resources divisions. His concern is with production activities.

President

The legal, accounting, human resources, and other departments report to the president.

In some companies, a single person serves as CEO, COO, and president. Our discussion will indicate that three individuals hold these positions and the CEO is the "top gun." The number of people who fill these positions depends on the size of the company and whether its operations are centralized or decentralized. Decentralized companies tend to operate with three distinctly different positions. The three functions can be combined more easily in a centralized company. As a variation, a company may have a CEO and president; the president may also serve as COO.

Executive Ethics

In recent years, several large companies toppled because of the activities of greedy, dishonest executives and their staffs. The CEOs of various companies such as Enron, WorldCom, and Tyco were convicted of serious crimes and sentenced to prison. Their conduct had ruinous consequences for employees and shareholders. They had the talent and knowledge to run their companies well and did so early in their careers. At some point, greed or other motivation led them to travel a different road. Money and power can make people believe they can get away with anything. Dishonest CEOs are not new. Unfortunately, they have the power to wreck an operation (and employee retirement

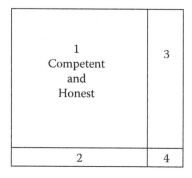

Figure 14.3 CEO classifications. The chart is drawn approximately to scale.

plans) in a very short time. This is not meant as criticism of CEOs in general. Most of them are intelligent, honest, and work hard in the interests of their companies and the shareholders.

CEO Classifications

The recent scandals involving prominent executives led us to classify them as shown in Figure 14.3.

Category 1: Competent and Honest—Obviously, this type of CEO is the best for any company and little comment is needed. Many competent and honest CEOs worked their way up to executive level and run their companies well.

Category 2: Competent and Dishonest—This is the most dangerous type of CEO. He knows the techniques of cheating and how to hide his activities from shareholders and the government. A competent but dishonest CEO can bleed a company by setting up fake subsidiaries, failing to reveal excessive company debts, and granting himself and hand-picked board members huge salaries and bonuses. The excessive payments to board members coerce them into following the CEO's direction instead of exercising unbiased judgment.

Category 3: Incompetent and Honest—Category 3 is undesirable but rates second best among the four categories. If such a CEO is sharp enough to select an effective and honest management team, the team will advance the company. Unfortunately, most competent managers don't want to work for an incompetent executive unless they have the freedom to run their areas effectively and help the company prosper.

Category 4: Incompetent and Dishonest—CEOs who are incompetent are dangerous, but only temporarily. Like a Category 4 hurricane, these CEOs wreak havoc and destruction for a time and then move. They cause a lot of damage in a short time but their tenures are short. They are not as dangerous as Category 2 CEOs.

CEOs and Communication

If you ask a chief executive officer if he wants to know what's going on in his company, his answer will always be, "Yes, of course." Despite the universal answer about knowing what's going on, why do many executives and managers appear oblivious to the constructive comments of their employees? See Figure 14.4 for a typical gap in the communication process. Who's correct? Why does management say one thing and the line workers say something else? Both think they are correct.

THERE SEEMS TO BE A GIGANTIC GAP IN THE COMMUNICATION PROCESS.
What occurred in the black box that changed the message 180 degrees?

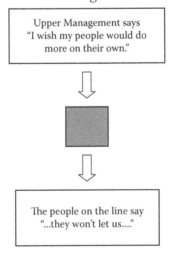

Figure 14.4 Communications paradox.

An effective CEO must get out of the office and observe activities first hand. That's the only way to acquire the accurate information you need to make important decisions.

Find out how your customers are treated to get genuine knowledge that will enable you to help your customers and grow your company. If you are the CEO of an airline, skip your personal jet. Buy your tickets and fly coach coast-to-coast with layovers. If you run a hotel chain, make your own reservations via the Internet or telephone and book an average room. Experience what your customers experience. Then you'll really know whether they are treated well or if it's time to make policy changes.

If you are out of town, call your office on the same number customers use instead of calling your secretary on your private line. See whether you are routed around or put on "hold" for an extended time. Call your customer service number (the one customers call when they have problems) and find out how they're treated. This may be the reason your competition is gaining an edge. Do you need a huge staff of assistants to give you second-hand information when you can easily get valid information directly? No duty can be more important than genuinely assessing customer satisfaction. Without customers you have no business. You can acquire some vital information simply by making a few phone calls.

Defining Your Business

Every company should periodically ask, "What business are we in?" This may sound simplistic but the answer is sometimes overlooked. The classic answer is, "We are in business to make money." But that does not truly answer the question, particularly in the modern era of diversification. Companies now acquire businesses of which they have little or no knowledge, then sell the businesses after incurring losses, realizing too late that they lacked the necessary expertise. It is vital to understand what business you are in.

As an exercise, pretend you are running Kodak and ask yourself what business are you in. Very little camera film is sold now because of advances in the photography field. Which business or combination of the businesses listed do you think Kodak is in?

- Film
- Videotape
- Image reproduction
- Image transmission
- Other businesses

The answers can be found on the Kodak website: www.kodak.com. Check the websites of other large companies. In the pharmaceutical field, check Johnson & Johnson (www.jnj.com). In addition to their various businesses, you will note their commitments in the areas of corporate responsibility and environmental sustainability. Select other companies in which you have an interest and look at their websites to determine their business and other activities. We discussed executive management teams earlier in this chapter. Review information about the backgrounds and affiliations of the management teams and boards of large companies. A board of directors should consist of people with excellent professional and personal reputations and superb perceptive, analytical, and decision making skills that will drive a company forward.

If you're a shareholder in a large public corporation, determine whether the management controls the stock by owning most of it. If that is the case, your votes as a shareholder will not count. While management may claim to be motivated by majority control, the company will use your money to play a game with a deck stacked against you. Own stock only in companies in which stockholders have the ability to remove management that does not work effectively.

If you get in your car and drive around aimlessly without a destination, you're wasting time and money. You have to know where to go and how to get there. If you don't have those facts, how will you know when you arrive? A start-up business frequently tries to "be all things to all people." That never works. Define your product, your business, and your customers, and stick with that until you succeed. The act of defining your business will channel your thinking in the right direction.

Goal Setting and Strategic Planning

In Chapter 1 and in the section above, we briefly discussed planning as a means to a successful business. Let's look now at the five fundamental steps in planning:

- Determine where you want to go.
- Decide what you need to get there.
- Make the decision.
- Implement the decision.
- Monitor feedback.

You may have heard of a WOTS UP analysis in relation to assessing an enterprise's capabilities and limitations in preparation of a strategic plan. WOTS UP is an acronym for weaknesses, opportunities, threats, and strengths underlying planning. It's clever and correct, but it's also incomplete. We will discuss an outline for a strategic plan, but before that some relevant points should be covered.

A strategic plan can cover any time span, but it normally covers a five-year period. This does not mean that it is prepared and not looked at again for five years! If no strategic activities are pursued for five years, you may not have a plan—or a company—to look at. You should review a strategic plan quarterly, monitor progress, and update the plan if required. After a review, you may determine that a new plan should be drawn up before the five years elapse because of changes in your business area or economic conditions. You must accommodate your plan to changes. Periodic reviews will determine whether you continue according to your plan or revise it.

In our example strategic plan, the research and development is included as an individual item. You may choose to highlight another department, or more departments, or no department. You may select fewer items in your plan. The example shown is generic and covers an entire company; your plan must suit your operation and may be designed for a division or department. For example, you may prepare a three-year plan for a sales department. Here are the usual components of a strategic plan:

- Preface
- Mission
- Objectives

- Threats and opportunities
- Weaknesses and strengths
- Growth
- Buildings and equipment
- Personnel
- Research and development
- Closing comments

Preface

The preface section should require only a paragraph or two and note the time period, for example:

"This plan covers ABC Company for the years 2010 through 2015. It should be specific enough to delineate direction, but not so specific as to limit the freedom of management. Because internal and external environments are continually changing, the plan should not be regarded as unalterable; it should be reviewed regularly and changed whenever the need arises.

The preface simply notes the period covered. The company reserves the right to alter this plan as the company and economy change."

Mission

The mission should discuss your primary products, intended rate of growth, comparison to previous results, and future plans. A single paragraph should be sufficient.

Objectives

Your objectives should be specific, for example:

1. Achieve a minimum 15% pre-tax profit.
2. Achieve a minimum 15% return on average gross assets (ROAGA).
3. Maintain a prominent public image in the community.

4. Maintain our present market share of 25%.

The objectives should be stated clearly in one or two lines each. They should be easy to measure, and the levels should be both optimistic and realistic. Don't get carried away with elaborate statements that may not be practical. A strategic plan should include attainable goals.

Threats and Opportunities

Threats   Depending on your product or service, threats could include potential product liability, government regulation, difficulties obtaining certain raw materials, or other factors that may affect the company or department. Discuss the effects the company can expect from the threats noted. And be aware that a threat can also serve as an opportunity; see the section below.

Opportunities   Use this section to lessen the impacts of threats. For example, product liability issues can become positive factors if you believe your company produces a safer product than competitors make. Another example of an opportunity is heavy customer reliance on your company for technical service that may lead to expansion of existing accounts.

Weaknesses and Strengths

Weaknesses
1. Lack of definitive measures of productivity
2. Few or no patented products; copying by competitors can be done with relative ease
3. Little experience or expertise in a field the company wants to enter

Strengths
1. Considerable knowledge, experience, and technical expertise in primary field of endeavor; leadership in the field
2. Strong market knowledge
3. Modern equipment in a new plant

Growth

The discussion of growth factors should cover issues such as production, assets, sales, profits, and other areas of expansion. The following text samples show how brief statements may be used effectively.

Production—"We will grow when Plant 4 goes onstream next year. We intend to maintain productivity from every square foot of manufacturing area and are presently studying the repositioning of workflow in all our plants."

Assets—"Two new large manufacturing machines, each capable of producing 20 items per hour, are budgeted for purchase next year. This will expand our current production rate of 10 items per hour."

Sales—"We anticipate sales growth of 15% per year based on increase in existing customer needs and the expansion of their product lines."*

Profits—"The increase in profits will be commensurate with increased sales and we expect profits to grow at a rate of 15% pre-tax. As we expand into international markets, we expect greater profits."

Buildings and Equipment (Optional Section)

Buildings and equipment are usually treated separately. Here are suggestions you might use.

Buildings—Discuss any relevant building or site issues in this section. You might list their functions, ages, and any planned expansions or improvements.

Equipment—Listing equipment used in manufacturing or research may give you a picture of where you are and where you want to go. Determine equipment status—is it new, well maintained, or in need of replacement?

---

* This type of statement is relevant if your company sells products for further manufacture through business-to-business (B to B) sales. If you sell your product to the final consumer, the sales section would contain wording appropriate to the particular consumer market.

Personnel

Future staffing, additions, training and other personnel matters should be discussed in this section. Here are examples.

Existing Personnel—"At this time we believe we have highly qualified individuals in most sections of the administrative, technical, and manufacturing areas."

Training—"We shall, through liaison with human resource development, continue to provide training to existing personnel. As individual assignments expand or as persons transfer from one assignment to another, if a need for training is determined to exist, it will be provided."

New Personnel—"We strive to attract above-average people regardless of age, race, sex, color, creed, or national origin."

Intentions—"We plan to keep our pay scales and fringe benefits above average in each area in which we operate. We intend to provide clean, comfortable, and safe working conditions for all employees. We will have employee–management meetings to discuss mutual problems and exchange ideas, and we will encourage participation in company-sponsored affairs. We intend to provide an atmosphere in which all employees can use their talents and abilities to the fullest extent possible. We will do this by determining, through observation and through our human resources department, what is needed to satisfy the work needs of our employees."

Research and Development

Below is a sample statement for use in operations where research and development are integral activities.

"We shall continue to maintain our emphasis on research and development efforts by carefully observing market needs and by allotting funds and personnel to research and development efforts. These efforts will be especially important as we pursue new areas for diversification. Another aspect of research and development is equally important: the dissemination of research findings to other personnel, the implementation of research findings to the production area, and eventual use in the marketplace. We shall also, with the help of our human resource department, foster a 'research and development thinking' attitude in employees outside the research and development area so that they will continually ask, 'How can we do it better?' This is a question that should be present all the time."

Closing Comments

Obviously, closing comments must be relevant to your product or service, past achievements and future goals. Here is an example summary.

"It is believed that the contents of this document will explain what we anticipate doing in the next five years and how we intend to achieve it. As we plan for the next five years, the key issues are to prepare the best plan possible based on current conditions, monitor our progress in meeting the plan, and modifying it whenever necessary based on changes in the internal or external environments."

Surely, a five-year plan that is not monitored for compliance will become stale and useless. Regular monitoring and modification will ensure that strategic plans will remain current and help a division or company achieve its goals. Efforts must be made to measure productivity accurately. "Productivity" is a key word in modern industry. Using the word is one thing; measuring it is another. Productivity may be stated as a ratio of sales to the number of employees, profit dollars divided by the number of employees, or number of units shipped per square foot of production area. Look into these various methods to determine the best ways to measure—and continually improve—productivity.

Summarizing the Strategic Plan

Every strategic plan is broken into categories appropriate for a particular operation. Some of those cited above will be optional for some companies and essential for others. You may wonder how your company will implement ideas discussed in a strategic plan. The answer lies in the goals you want for yourself and your company. You may choose to have a shorter plan or may decide to be more direct. The primary point is that the plan should suit your needs and be modified as required. A basic plan could be covered in a few pages without the need for long descriptions or numerous graphs. The United States Constitution is not a lengthy document and has survived more than 200 years. It serves as a good example of a long-range plan that includes provisions for amendments.

The most important element in your plan is *honesty*. Of course, *accuracy* is almost as important, but any inaccuracies can be corrected promptly if you review your strategic plan regularly. If your plan is not honest, perhaps because you considered readers' wishes instead of reality, you will be following a faulty plan that will not meet your needs or achieve success.

Keep in mind the difference between *strategy* and *tactics*. Strategy defines overall philosophy; tactics encompass individual means of accomplishing goals. As each division or department fashions its own strategic plan after the company's primary plan, the individual plans will include more tactics that will define how the individual units of divisions or departments will accomplish their goals. Everything then blends upward to the overall company goals.

If you can read and understand strategic plans, you are ready to prepare your own plan based on what you want from your career. The exercise will be helpful on a personal level—it is difficult to pursue a successful career without a plan.

Management Styles

Some management techniques are effective; some are far from good. We present both types here for purposes of learning and comparison.

Management by Hiding (MBH)—As its name implies, the manager who practices this technique believes problems will work themselves out if he cannot be found. He will be present to take credit for accomplishments of his staff but generally he lacks the ability to face problems that may arise. You don't want to practice MBH or work for a manager who does.

Ostrich Management—This is very similar to MBH. However, while the ostrich sticks his head in the sand and believes that he is hiding, this manager keeps on the move, and while he does not have a secret hiding place that no one knows about, he cannot be pinned down to answer questions or be faced with problems. He sticks his head in the sand along any part of the beach when asked a question he doesn't want to, or lacks the nerve to, answer.

Absentee Management—The absentee manager is never available. Many good managers are required to travel a lot, but the absentee manager travels constantly. No one knows why he travels, where he goes, how long he will be away, or when he will return. He is "out" in more ways than one.

Mushroom Management—This technique is based figuratively on the principles used to raise mushrooms: keep employees in the dark and throw manure on them.

Management by Objectives (MBO)—This is a productive management technique. A manager and employee meet and agree on the objectives the employee should achieve in a certain period, usually a year. The biggest problem related to MBO is inflexibility, i.e., during the projected year, businesses, markets, and staffs change, but the objectives haven't. MBO works very well when flexibility is incorporated via regular reviews to adjust the objectives to conditions inside and outside the company.

Management by Common Sense and Nerve (MBCSN)—This principle coupled with getting out among customers and employees is the best form of management. Essentially, this type of manager does not sit at a desk behind a pile of computer printouts and spend days analyzing statistics. He talks to employees at all levels, discusses situations and exchanges ideas with other managers, uses common sense, and has the nerve to make the proper decisions. This obviously is the type of manager you want to be and the type of manager you want to work for. This type of manager will help a corporation progress and meet its goals.

Common sense and nerve, combined with confidence and a pleasant personality, have traditionally been the best and most effective traits for a manager. In fact, these four attributes support and strengthen each other. Confidence and common sense lead to a pleasant personality and equip an individual with nerve. MBH and other ineffective techniques were discussed here to enable you to recognize and avoid them. Obviously, MBO and MBCSN are the styles recommended for any management level.

15

BUSINESS AND TECHNICAL RELATIONSHIPS

Symbiosis to Maximize Profits

At times, company business and technical functions seem to occupy two different worlds. A company that requires technical functions cannot maximize its profits when these two areas are so far apart and don't work together effectively. How can they be doing good jobs for the company if they're out of sync? Business and technical functions are not different planets operating where they choose within the company orbit. They must be kept in alignment.

The two areas may not be at odds; they simply may not understand each other. How then do you get them to work together more effectively? The first step is to have them understand each other, but this is easier said than done. The process is similar to convincing people to see other views in an effort to reach understanding, if not agreement. It is satisfying and rewarding to learn to deal with other people. Similarly, understanding and cooperating with another function in a company leads to appreciation, then possibly agreement, and ultimately a symbiotic relationship that will lead to maximizing profits.

Effective communication plays a major role in aiding understanding of various company functions and enhancing their ability to work together. That subject and other people skills are covered in Chapter 16.

In some companies, technical and business functions "get along well," often in small companies where people see each other daily. In larger companies, maintaining relationships through education and well-planned, constructive meetings of the various disciplines ensures that this mutual understanding and appreciation continues. Proper interdepartmental relationships can be established and maintained when all parties have some understanding of each other. Table 15.1 illustrates weak and/or undesirable relationships (little understanding)

Table 15.1 Weak or Undesirable Relationships

SUBJECT	TYPICAL COMMENT					
	R & D	MARKETING	LEGAL	SALES	MANUFACTURING	FINANCE
New product design	This is a great new product. Let's hope that sales knows how to do a good job here so we can all get rich.	R & D did it again. They invented something no one will buy.	Wow! Those R & D people left this product open to liability suits. They never think of the legal end when they design something.		They did it again! We have to retool the entire production line.	
Business trips to customers	We'd sell a lot more product if sales took us and our technical service people along on business trips.		Don't let them talk to customers; they'll promise them anything!	Now if those science people will just invent something else and do their jobs, we'll sell the products.		We're spending a lot of money sending unnecessary people on trips.
New production equipment					At last.	Do they really need that?
Advertising and promotion	The company should spend a bundle on this because it's so good.		We'd better be very careful what we say. We can be sued if we say the wrong thing.		Who cares!	Let's be careful what we spend.
New product testing		Let's get the data the minute it's available and run to customers with it.		Let's get the data the minute it's available and run to customers with it.		

among typical company areas. Each area exhibits a different view because it focuses inward and fails to see the need for interaction. You are invited to imagine what comments on the part of your company operations would fit into the empty areas of the table. You can devise a similar chart or copy this one. You may find that various departments or divisions of your company have very interesting opinions, and you can use such information to see how you might bring about better agreement that will lead to better workflow, more and better products, and more profits.

Table 15.2 portrays good working relationships among company areas. It would be great if your relationships were similar to those shown in the table. Try the exercise above with Table 15.2. If your company relationships lie somewhere between the extremes of Tables 15.1 and 15.2 and lean toward the latter, your divisions probably get along well.

The example below depicts what can happen when coordination between departments appears good on the surface but is unsatisfactory. The incident really happened and such problems continue to occur in this and other industries with other products. The industry involved in the incident manufactured rubber stoppers of the types used to seal vials of flu vaccine. Doctors withdraw vaccines from such vials for injection into patients. The rubber stoppers are very carefully designed so that little or no material used in their manufacture will extract into the injectable solution and cause harm to patients.

A customer of the rubber stopper maker, a major pharmaceutical manufacturer, was interested in a new stopper formula in development. The salesman who serviced the pharmaceutical company paid frequent visits to the research department to see what innovations he could take to his customer. A stopper manufacturer makes money by selling a lot of product. A typical stopper may cost about five cents to manufacture. If a company sells them for nine cents each, the profit on a monthly order from a single customer for five million stoppers is handsome and we can assume the company has other customers.

The research and development department developed a new stopper formula that exhibited the required chemical properties. The research people went to the pilot plant to procure stoppers made from the new formulation. The pilot plant sorted out the imperfect stoppers and produced a box of a few hundred good looking stoppers, without

Table 15.2 Desirable Relationships

SUBJECT	R & D	MARKETING	LEGAL	SALES	MANUFACTURING	FINANCE
				TYPICAL COMMENT		
New product design	Let's meet with manufacturing to make sure we design something they can produce.		Let's talk about this design thoroughly before hitting the market with it.	R & D listens to us and I believe we're coming out with a new product soon.		
Business trips to customers	We appreciate the opportunities to meet with customers.	The research people are a big help in explaining technicalities to customers.	We are always cautious but we have confidence in our technical people.			Some of those R & D people really seem to understand costs; they don't always expect to fly first class.
New production equipment	Good! Manufacturing is going to make the products we invented.	Good! Manufacturing is going to make the products we're marketing.			This will help us maintain full employment and produce quality products.	
Advertising and promotion		Working with R & D helps us design promotional strategies.	We may have to be conservative but we trust our technical and marketing groups.		Let's sell a lot of product so we can keep the plant running with full employment.	
New product testing			We're confident that our product is safe.	We have good data that tells us and our customers about the product.	Production is running smoothly, thanks to advanced testing.	A worthwhile investment; it will save us money in the long run.

mentioning that *for every good stopper produced, nine imperfect ones had to be thrown out!* This represents a 90% reject level, or discarding 900 of every 1000 stoppers produced. Producing stoppers at a cost of five cents each is good, assuming no rejects. Producing only one good stopper of every ten escalates the production cost to fifty cents per stopper. This information had not yet been conveyed from the pilot plant to the research department. The salesman visited the pilot plant, saw the good stoppers, and delivered 100 samples to his customer. The customer liked the stoppers and after accelerated testing of the samples, placed a very large order.

Now, take a close look at the situation. The salesman had an order for 10 million stoppers he thought cost five cents each and sold for nine cents. In reality, he was selling for nine cents new stoppers that cost fifty cents to make. The salesman had to admit to the customer that he acted prematurely and that the formulation was not yet ready to sell. The customer had almost set up a production schedule for sealing one of its products in vials using this new stopper. Had that occurred, it would have cost the customer tens of thousands of dollars to retool its equipment and the stopper manufacturer would have been expected to absorb some or all of that cost because it promised to deliver the new product.

This is a genuine example of a problem arising from a lack of communication. Be careful to prevent the transmittal of piecemeal or incorrect information from one department to another before all the fine points are worked out. Have effective communications among the various departments if you want to make and sell your product or service efficiently. It is easy for a salesperson to talk about a product; it is not so easy to deliver what he promised, as promised, and on time. When communications about costs, availability, and production issues flow well interdepartmentally, a product or service can be provided at a convenience to the customer and a profit to you.

The reverse situation can also occur. Perhaps a product is ready to go to the market and company management is timid about introducing it until it is tested ad infinitum. A good case in point concerns a harness maker in 1900 who wanted to make the finest harness available. He isolated himself in his workshop for 3 years to develop the harness; his wife even delivered his meals to his workshop. He had made several high quality harnesses but continued to strive for perfection. When he emerged from his workshop after three years, he was surprised at the sight he beheld. People no longer rode horses! The contraption now called a car was used for transport and people no longer needed harnesses. This continues to happen today. Management may have a good product, but if it delays getting its product to the market promptly, a competitor whose product may be inferior may capture the market share.

These two examples clearly show that *timeliness* is a key factor along with the proper dissemination of information within a company. Relationships among departments and areas tend to be close when a company starts up, but may diminish as a company grows. Remember the example of a mobile used in Chapter 1—displacement of one segment forced the entire mobile to shift to regain equilibrium. An unexpected shift causes a great disruption, but a planned shift should be effectively accommodated by all divisions or departments.

The best way to avoid any problems is to consistently demand accurate and effective communication among divisions. More will be said about communication in the next chapter. For now, keep in mind that communications among the various functions facilitate introduction of products to the market and modifications of existing products. Effective interdepartmental communications ultimately lead to the generation of profits for the company.

16
PEOPLE SKILLS

How to Get Along with Others
(The Most Important Chapter in This Book)

Introduction

It's an established fact that as people move up the ladder of success they rely more and more on their "people skills," (i.e., ability to get along with others) than on their technical competence. Actually, people move up faster and achieve more success as they rely more heavily on skills in working with people. Several years ago, one of the University of Michigan graduate schools asked over 1100 executives which courses they felt prepared a student for business leadership. The most common response, with a rating of 71%, was business communication; the second highest rating of 64% was attributed to finance (Chapter 4).

In his 1987 book called *Growing a Business*, Paul Hawken discusses business plans and marketing plans. In an explanation of the competitive analysis section of a marketing plan, Paul says, "Ironically, the reader will learn more from this section about the character of the writer than about the character of the competition." Thus, the communication between writer and reader conveys more than what the writer intends to present about the marketing plan; it communicates something about the writer to the reader.

Doesn't a painting in a museum communicate something about the painter? Do depressed people paint depressing scenes and happy people paint happy scenes? What you produce, whether a painting, song, poem, or marketing plan, reveals more than your fundamental message. You communicate information about yourself.

A way of recognizing the importance of people skills is to remember that some of the best events ensue when someone says "yes" to something you propose. Conversely, some of the biggest disappointments occur when you receive a "no." Isn't it logical to learn how to persuade people to give you the answer you want?

Getting along with others covers a lot of territory. You want to get along with others in family life, at work, at civic functions and social events, and in many other places and situations. In the early 1900s, Andrew Carnegie paid Charles Schwab $1,000,000 a year to manage a steel company. Charles Schwab knew how to get a job done and readily admitted that his ability to deal with people contributed to his success. In the early 1900s, $1,000,000 a year was a very large salary even for an executive of a steel company.

You have to have some knowledge about your primary field of endeavor. However, the ability to have people do what you want and like it is a talent that will bring much success both in personal satisfaction and professional advancement. According to Chapter 19, "Starting Your Own Business," knowing the product and knowing the customer are the two most important assets you need when you want to start a business. That fact doesn't minimize the need for people skills. Besides reading relevant literature, how do you think you acquire knowledge about your product and your customer? By utilization of your people skills!

Getting along with others involves, from a management view, persuading them to do what you want them to do and having them like it. This admittedly is easier in some situations than in others. In some cases, it requires more effort and is not completely successful, but it is still the best policy.

Listening

Listening is part of the communications process. It is so important, it is considered as a separate topic within this chapter. It has been said that you have two ears and one mouth and should use them proportionately. That means you should spend two-thirds of your communication time listening. This equates to twice as much listening as speaking. (Listening to yourself talk counts as talking, not listening.) Listening is more than simply not speaking. It includes reading what

Figure 16.1 Has this ever happened to you?

other people have written before you reply. For brevity here we will use the terms *listening* and *speaking*, but these terms also apply to the written word. Before describing the advantages of listening in more detail, let's take a few typical questions that have been asked about listening skills and their answers.

Q: When I am in a one-to-one conversation, I have difficulty in knowing what to do with my hands. What do I do?

A: All you have to do is place one hand somewhere and know that it is there, e.g., on the arm of a chair, or on your knee. The other hand will take care of itself and won't get you in trouble. Fidgeting often occurs when both hands are moving at the same time.

Q: Where do I look when I am in a conversation?

A: When you are talking, look into the other person's eyes. And when he is talking, look into his mouth because that is where the sound comes from. You will find it easy to speak and listen if you follow those pointers. Of course, if he is showing you a document, look at the document.

Q: I feel a little uneasy when speaking to supervisors or superiors in business. What do I do?

A: Carry a tablet, manila folder, or portfolio folder. This keeps your hands occupied and gives you something to write on if you must take notes. It conveys your interest to the other person. Do not immediately start writing copious notes. This will detract from your listening and you may miss important information. Even if you take no notes, the tablet will have served a purpose by showing your interest while allowing you to look at the person speaking and to listen to that person.

People who speak to us sometimes have a characteristic such as a heavy accent that can distract us from listening well. Has this ever happened to you? Have you ever "turned off" a person because he or she had an accent and it was too much trouble to listen? Does the presence of an accent mean that what the person says is not important? You should try to listen. The person knows he has an accent and that you have trouble understanding him. Say something like, "I am interested in what you have to say but I am having trouble understanding you. Could you repeat that a little more slowly?" The person now knows that you want to hear him and that you believe what he has to say is important. He is not going to walk away in disgust. He is going to speak slowly and more clearly so that you can understand his message.

This approach also works with people who have speech impediments, people who are speaking to you in a noisy environment, and in other situations that require the efforts of all parties in a conversation. The other person knows about the distraction. Simply let him know that you want to hear what he has to say and ask him to speak more slowly, speak more clearly, or move away from the background noise. He will appreciate your giving him the opportunity to be understood.

Certain keys to effective listening will help you develop good listening habits. They are listed in Table 16.1. Review the table and attempt to assess your listening skills. Table 16.2 is another type of assessment consisting of a series of questions and a scoring mechanism. Few virtues are more highly prized and less practiced than good listening. The

Table 16.1   Ten Keys to Effective Listening

TEN KEYS TO EFFECTIVE LISTENING	THE BAD LISTENER	THE GOOD LISTENER
Find areas of interest	Tunes out dry subjects	Looks for opportunities: "What's in it for me?" "What can I learn here?"
Judge content, not delivery	Tunes out if delivery is poor	Judges content, skips delivery errors
Hold your fire	Tends to argue	Doesn't judge until comprehension is complete
Listen for ideas	Listens for facts	Listens for central themes
Be flexible	Takes intensive notes using only one system	Takes few notes: uses various systems (charts, text, drawing) depending on speaker (also depends on listener's preference)
Work at listening	Shows no energy output; fakes attention	Works hard; exhibits active body state
Resist distractions	Is easily distracted	Fights or avoids distractions; tolerates bad habits; knows how to concentrate
Exercise your mind	Resists difficult expository material; seeks light, recreational material	Uses heavier material as mental exercise
Keep your mind open	Reacts to emotional words	Interprets emotional words
Focus on fact; thought is faster than speech	Tends to daydream	Challenges; anticipates; mentally summarizes; weighs evidence; listens to tone of voice

checklist in Table 16.2 will help you evaluate your listening habits. The ten keys of Table 16.1 constitute a guide to better listening and can help you develop better listening habits that could last a lifetime. Consider an interesting paradox. Most people want to know what is going on in the world but are too busy talking to listen. Keep in mind that in your business and technical activities, you make decisions most effectively by evaluating information, and you acquire information by listening.

Table 16.2 Rating Listening Ability

WHEN TAKING PART IN AN INTERVIEW OR CONFERENCE, DO YOU:	USUALLY	SOMETIMES	SELDOM
1. Prepare physically by sitting facing the speaker and making sure you can hear?			
2. Watch the speaker as you listen?			
3. Decide from the speaker's appearance and delivery whether what he or she has to say is worthwhile?			
4. Listen primarily for ideas and underlying feelings?			
5. Determine your own bias, if any and try to allow for it?			
6. Keep your mind on what the speaker is saying?			
7. Interrupt immediately if you hear a statement you feel is wrong?			
8. Make sure before answering that you understand the other person's view?			
9. Try to have the last word?			
10. Make a conscious effort to evaluate the logic and credibility of what you hear?			

Scoring Results: Questions 1, 2, 4, 5, 6, 8, 10: 10 points for "usually," 5 for "sometimes," 0 for "seldom." Questions 3, 7, 9: 0 points for "usually," 5 for "sometimes," 10 for "seldom."

Interpretation: A score below 70 indicates you have developed poor listening habits; a score from 70 to 85 suggests that you listen well but could improve; a score of 90+ means you are an excellent listener.

Communications

Our planet sustains six billion people and sooner or later you will have to communicate with some of them. This section explains why it is necessary to communicate effectively. We will look at examples of communication in your daily work, discuss some rules of communication, and make you aware of communications that may be misunderstood. We will also look at ways to improve your communication skills. As you progress through your career, good work alone will not project you to stardom. Your abilities must be communicated to the proper persons inside and outside your company. You should communicate effectively for two reasons: (1) efficiency in your assigned work and (2) advertising your talents to others. In essence, good communication produces good public relations (PR).

Advertising your talents to others is not an ego trip. It simply means doing good work and having the proper people realize that. The technique works in both directions. If you are on your way up the corporate ladder, you want the people above you to know what talents you have. By writing good reports and speaking at conferences, you communicate the results of your good work. If you are already an executive, you want to communicate your thoughts and directions to your staff. You might say that you wouldn't be an executive if you didn't have good communication ability. While that may be true, it is not uncommon for managers to realize their communication skills are not adequate. Communications in your daily work can involve writing reports, memoranda, and e-mails, talking by phone and in person, speaking to small groups at meetings, making presentations to large audiences, and writing articles and books.

One fundamental point for a communicator to remember is that *the responsibility for communicating rests with the person trying to communicate!* To cite an extreme example, assume you were raised in the United States and English is your native language. You are speaking to a group of persons who speak German. You cannot simply say what you want to say in English, in the belief that if they want to hear you, they will learn English; they may even know English. However, if you really want them to understand, speak in German or have a translator by your side. Admittedly, this is a non-typical case, but it does demonstrate the point of taking responsibility for your communications, even when someone else is speaking and you are listening, as noted earlier.

Here are some examples of miscommunications. Did you ever have any similar communication experiences?

Example 1—Two people are at a race track. One person says, "I know the jockey riding horse number 3 in this race." The other person makes a big bet on horse number 3, which comes in last. The second person says, "I thought you said you knew the jockey." The first person replies, "That's right. I do. He's a real nice guy. He can't ride a horse very well, but he sure is a nice guy." Note that the first person never said the jockey could ride well. The second person arrived at a conclusion based on insufficient evidence and lost his bet.

Example 2—Two people are walking on a sidewalk and see a man in his 40s with dark hair. The first person says, "That looks like

George Clooney, the movie star." The other person answers, "That's not George Clooney." The first person says, "I know that's not George Clooney," and the second person replies, "But you just said it was." The first person responds, "No, I didn't. I only said that person looked like George Clooney." And you get the idea. This situation is not uncommon when someone uses a phrase like "looks like" and another person misinterprets it based on an assumption. Remember, in management and in communications, when you break down the word *assume* it makes an *ass* of *u* and *me*. While you should listen to what people say, you should be just as aware of what they *don't say.*

I know that you believe you understand what you think I said, but I am not sure you realize that what you heard is not what I meant.

Example 3—I received tickets to a football game and suggested that my son meet me outside the stadium near a football player statue that is 18-feet high. This way we could meet before the game even though 65,000 other people were entering the stadium. Fortunately, we remembered that a statue of a runner was at one end of the stadium and a statue of a kicker was at the other end. Had we not remembered that fact or failed to clarify it, we might have waited at opposite ends of the stadium.

Example 4—Assume a laboratory occupies a building a mile away from the marketing department. The laboratory director called the marketing director and suggested a meeting for the following Tuesday at 8 a.m. in the gold conference room. At the appointed time, each group went to the gold conference room in its own building. They waited, and tempers began to flare; each group thought the other group did not bother to appear on time. Fortunately, the laboratory director called the marketing director. They realized that there was a communication error and agreed on which conference room to meet in at 9 a.m. This may seem like a small error, but it meant a lot of nonproductive time spent by high-priced talent. Further delay would have required marketing people to rearrange their flight schedules, incurring additional expense.

Example 5—One person believes he is complimenting another by saying, "That's a nice tie." The other person thinks, "I really don't like this tie and I'm wearing it only because my spouse gave it to me and I don't want any hurt feelings. The person complimenting me has poor taste." This is perhaps an extreme case; however, if the first person said "I like that tie," thus stating his own feelings, the compliment would have been accepted much more readily.

In situations like these, a little forethought would have prevented any confusion and negative reactions.

Have you ever confused people without trying to do so? It's easy to confuse people and just as easy to simplify what you are trying to say if you give it some thought. This happens a lot when a person is not at his desk and you are leaving word with an assistant who (1) may not know you, (2) takes your message on a 3-inch square pad or enters it into a computer, (3) has taken 20 other messages for her absent boss. You say that most places have voice mail these days? Yes, most do. However, when reaching some of the top level executives at large companies you may find that if you call a direct line, they answer their own phones or their assistants answer for them.

Voice mail is fine when set up properly. Some systems are professional; others are so convoluted or silly that they present a poor image. Unfortunately, these types are usually installed on customer service lines. "All representatives are busy at the moment" may mean the company has only one representative. After dissatisfied customers tell others and sales decrease, management will blame "the market" or "the economy," without considering the true cause: inadequate customer service.

If you wonder why your phone calls are not returned after you leave a message, it may have been misunderstood. When you leave a voice message, speak clearly and give the following information:

1. Hello (that's a good start)
2. The day, date, and time of day (including time zone, if appropriate)
3. Who you are (your name and the name of your company)
4. The purpose of this call (request for information, delivery of information, whatever)
5. State your own phone number and/or e-mail address clearly, twice
6. Thank You
7. Your name again

This sequence above can be completed usually in 30 to 40 seconds. If you are not prepared to leave this information quickly, don't make the call. You want to be sure that you deliver a clear message and convey your information.

Using your cell phone, call your home or office and leave a message for yourself. When you hear your recorder pick up you will know how your recorded message sounds. When you leave a message and play it back, you will hear what you sound like. When you are satisfied, try it the other way; use your home or office phone to call your cell phone and evaluate your performance. If you want to hear good, concise accurate communication, listen to a typical conversation between a pilot and the air traffic controller. When the pilot initiates the conversation he calls the tower. The tower acknowledges and then the pilot says what he wants by following the rule of stating:

- Who you are
- Where you are
- What you want to do

It's that simple. Let's take an example of a Cessna Citation and the Philadelphia International Airport tower:

(When no one else is talking on the assigned frequency):
Philadelphia tower, this is Citation N-10704.
(Immediately, or a few seconds later):
Go ahead, 10704 (note that the tower dropped the "N").
The pilot responds:
10704 is 10 miles north at 10,000 feet. Request permission to transit your air space.
The tower responds:
Permission granted, 10704. Maintain altitude and transit air space.
The pilot responds:
10704 will maintain altitude and transit your air space. Thank you and good day.

It's that simple. It's clear and to the point. During this time the tower has also been observing the plane—and—others on the radar screen.

Table 16.3 Communication Without Words

GESTURE	MEANING
Hand wringing	Considering idea
Rubbing nose	Rejection, disagreement
Patting air	Approval
Steepling fingers	Feeling of superiority
Rubbing eyes	Inner desire not to see something that might change mind
Fingers interlocked, elbows on desk	Inward struggle to keep silent
Tugging shirt cuff	Self-satisfaction
Hitching trousers	Concern about making decision
Legs crossed, one foot swinging	Desire to walk away
Standing with arms crossed	Confident, possibly arrogant

Nonverbal Communications

Some people rely heavily on body language but interpretation should be "taken with a grain of salt." The gestures listed in Table 16.3 may indicate the meanings listed, but that is not necessarily the case. Remember that body language is observed during a conversation. If you are looking at that person's eyes or mouth, you should gain a feel for the flow of the conversation. And keep in mind that the other person may be reading your gestures.

Some words appear more favorable than other words. Table 16.4 lists "sweet and sour" words. You may think of others. Remember that the true meaning of a word comes out in the context in which it is

Table 16.4 Words: Sweet and Sour

MOST PEOPLE LIKE THESE WORDS	MOST PEOPLE DISLIKE THESE WORDS
advantage, appreciate, benefit, capable, confidence, conscientious, cooperation, courtesy, dependable, desirable, ease, economy, effective, efficient, energy, enthusiasm, genuine, helpful, honesty, honor, integrity, justice, kindness, loyalty, please, popularity, practical, prestige, progress, reliable, responsible, satisfactory, service, success, superior, useful, valuable, vigor, you, yours	abuse, alibi, allege, apology, beware, blame, cheap, commonplace, complaint, crisis, decline, discredit, dispute, exaggerate, extravagance, failure, fault, fear, fraud, hardship, ignorant, imitation, implicate, impossible, misfortune, negligent, opinionated, prejudiced, retrench, rude, squander, superficial, tardy, timid, unfair, unfortunate, unsuccessful, waste, worry, wrong

Table 16.5 Communication Media

TYPE	EFFECTIVENESS	EXAMPLES
Written, including e-mail and attachments	Most effective for transmitting lengthy and detailed material	Memoranda, charts, diagrams, bulletins, company newspapers; any information disseminated after proper security measures are in place
Oral	Most effective for communications requiring translation, explanations to clarify material for recipients with varying language skills, and when immediate feedback is desired	Meetings and conversations, telephone conversations, lectures, conferences
Multimedia, including videoconferencing allowing all parties to see and speak	Most effective in situations such as settling work disputes, communicating major policy changes, complying with government requirements, new product launches	Written and oral, written and visual, oral and visual, written and oral and visual

used. These tables, like other charts in this book and elsewhere convey data in its most simplistic form. You will be engaged in conversation (or writing) and you will use these as you see fit.

We have covered here much about verbal communication; written communication operates in parallel in the sense that you will listen twice as much as you speak, and read at least twice as much as you write. You should know when to use writing instead of verbal communication. Table 16.5 provides guidelines—not absolute instructions. When you want to convey information verbally or in writing to an individual or a large group, keep in mind three points:

- What do you want to say?
- To whom do you want to say it?
- Do you have their attention?

If you can answer those three fundamental questions before speaking or writing, your communications should be effective. Certainly, the probability of being understood is far greater than if you didn't answer those three questions. To improve your communications ability, here are some suggestions:

Be aware—This may be redundant but it is important. You must know what you want to say and know the backgrounds of your audience members. A scientist addressing people without scientific backgrounds must speak differently than he would talk to scientific colleagues.

Someone who doesn't have complete information may not see issues as clearly as you do—I have done volunteer work for Recording for the Blind, a nonprofit organization that helps visually impaired people. They subscribe to audio tapes and learn in that manner from the same books read by people who have sight. The organization is supported primarily by volunteers who record in a studio and the tapes are duplicated for distribution. I once attempted to describe a bar graph as part of my reading and said something like, "The blue line is about twice as high as the red line, which in turn is twice as high as the green line." Another volunteer enlightened me when she said, "Jim, that's okay for people who were once able to see, but what about the people who have never seen, and don't know one color from another?" This was a realization for me. After that conversation, I hope my efforts to communicate with visually impaired people significantly improved.

I included this story so that you will know, as you try to describe a chart, graph, or computer screen to someone on the phone across the country (who cannot see the chart or other item), that you must describe things in the necessary detail. Try this exercise. Select a page from a book, especially a page with a graph or chart, and try to describe it over the phone to a person who cannot see it. Ask for feedback.

Consider joining Toastmasters International to improve your public speaking skills—This organization (known as TM) has many local groups that meet regularly. The meetings run about an hour. Find a local group that meets at a convenient time. You can attend a few meetings as a guest before you will be asked to consider membership. The cost is about $60 annually (variable geographically) after an initial fee of about $20. In addition to covering administration costs, the annual fee includes a monthly *Toastmasters* magazine, which contains very good articles on speaking and listening.

Practice making presentations—Make short practice presentations to peers or friends or try practicing before an imaginary audience. You will find that vocalizing your thoughts clarifies your ideas and helps your delivery. If you plan to give a presentation in a conference room you have never seen, visit the room when it's empty, before the presentation, to "get the feel" from the front of the room and practice your introduction and maybe a minute or so of your presentation. You will feel far more comfortable when you make the presentation and deliver it more effectively.

Prepare a 30-second commercial—Whenever you have something to say verbally or in writing, try condensing your thoughts into a 30-second statement, even if you are scheduled to make a 30-minute presentation, and make the statement to an imaginary person or someone you know. If you can present your message in 30 seconds, you know your subject well and will have the essence of your presentation clearly in mind.

Smart on-the-job communication is not about writing more reports or drafting memos. It's about talking to people to build and sustain a two-way bridge of honest information exchange. The goal is to bring people separated by structural hierarchy together into the same boat to sail toward a common goal.

When Someone Points Out an Error You Made

This situation is worth mentioning because everyone occasionally makes an error. Many people react incorrectly. If someone points out an "error" you made, simply say something like "OK." Never respond by pointing out an error that person made. That will only divert his or her attention temporarily and lead to more "Well, you did..." statements, thus aggravating the situation.

If someone says, "You were supposed to call ABC enterprises and you forgot," answer, "Yes, but I'll take care of it." Do not say, "Well, last month you forgot to call XYZ" or "Yesterday you were late for a meeting." That type of response serves no useful purpose. At best, it wastes time. At worst, it starts an argument.

The "blame game" is present in industry, in family situations, and elsewhere. This simple scenario has wasted ridiculous amounts of time in business and in personal relations. Don't get caught in the game. Be smart and prevent blame statements from escalating into confrontations by addressing the issue without mentioning the other person's faults. This mechanism works wonders.

Navigating Two-Way Streets

Some people have to be reminded of the principle of the two-way street. *If you want someone to do something, you must provide adequate reason for the person to do so.* This is another way of saying that (usually) people don't do things unless they receive something in return. You must provide proper motivation for people to do what you want them to do. However, some people may not realize that when they deal with you.

There are those who only take and do not give, for example, customers who want discounts for no reason other than that they want them. They won't guarantee large volume purchases to qualify for discounts. Have you ever received requests for money from organizations simply because they asked for it without regard to your other obligations? If you give (to some of them) frequently, they feel they know you well enough to send you the forms to include their organization in your will.

All fair and honest persons know that people relationships in personal life and business involve doing things for others and receiving some type of return.

How to Lose Friends

Friends constitute an integral part of business and everyday living. Be careful in business not to bring up certain subjects and express opinions about them. Three subjects and your opinions about them should never be interjected into a conversation: religion, politics, and the other person's spouse and children. This is good advice in business and in your personal life. Hundreds of other subjects won't get you into trouble.

There is an important principle that works when lecturing to a large audience or when chatting with individuals: If you are not sure whether what you say will be offensive, the principle is: *When in doubt, leave it out.*

Everyone has opinions on numerous things. What some people were never taught—nor did they ever figure out—is that at times it is not smart to volunteer these opinions.

Negotiation

It has been said that in business you don't get what you deserve; you get what you negotiate.

We said earlier in this chapter that you communicate constantly. You also negotiate much of the time. You negotiate when you want to go to a ball game and your spouse wants to go to the opera. You negotiate when you drive your car on the entrance ramp to a freeway and you work your way into the traffic lane. Think of how many times during a day you negotiate for something, sometimes with people very close and also with people you don't know.

The object of negotiation is not to produce a winner and a loser or to work out a compromise. The win-lose result is obvious. The compromise requires one or more parties to give up something important and often produces a degree of dissatisfaction.

Negotiating, on the other hand, should produce a win–win situation in which both parties feel they received something they wanted and both are satisfied. Certain steps should be followed if you want to negotiate successfully.

Information Gathering

Before you negotiate, learn as much information as you can about the other party. Find out what that person really wants. Consider an employer negotiating with a person to be hired as an executive. The salary issue is obvious; everyone wants more income, but at some point increasing the salary figure has little effect. That is why, during negotiations for high positions, an employer will offer a "package." Membership in a country club is a good perquisite (perk). While it might cost $6,000, it may be more effective psychologically than a $20,000 salary increase. Remember, beyond a certain point, salary increases have little impact. The fact that the employer *gave* the country club membership to the new executive is more important than the executive's ability to purchase his own membership. Does this feed the ego? Of course it does.

How many times did people think you wanted one thing when you really wanted something else? In the case of purchasing a home, the seller wants a particular amount and the buyer wants to pay less than that amount. The negotiations open and can get lengthy. When the seller needs the money immediately and the buyer wants to pay no more than 90% of the asking price, negotiations may reach an impasse. In a different case, the parties may learn that the seller does not need the money immediately and the buyer wants a smaller monthly mortgage payment. Based on this new information, a mutually beneficial agreement may be reached. The seller could agree to a smaller down payment, allowing the buyer to meet the full price. Or, the seller might agree to delay the sale to receive the full asking price. Both parties acquired information and were in a position to reach an agreement.

Negotiators and Decision Makers

If more than one person is involved in negotiations on behalf of one party, don't assume that the person sitting at the head of the table is the decision maker or that all the people representing a company share decision making responsibilities equally. The real decision maker may sit on the sidelines and let assistants handle negotiations. You have to use your judgment in cases like this. You may note that the participants will look to one person to signal approval. If you don't think it is proper to ask who the primary decision maker is, you might say, "If we come to agreement on all the terms in this meeting, are you prepared to sign the contract now?" In this case, they will either say they can, or they should tell you that they have to take it up with higher authority. Once you find out who the decision maker is, direct all your activities toward that person.

Have Several Issues for Discussion

There is a tendency with many people to want to get to the bottom line fast and to do this by having only one single issue to discuss. Then, to their dismay, they find that they have left themselves no bargaining room. If you want to negotiate successfully, have your central issue "on the table" along with various other issues of lesser significance to you. Always be aware, of course, of what your primary issue is, and try to find out what the other person's primary issue is. By doing this you can "give up" some smaller issue, or part of your stance on an issue, to the other person. This shows that you are willing to give something to that person and, in turn, he will be willing to give some things to you and to modify some of his more rigid positions. This takes time, of course, but it leads to a successful result.

As an example, if labor is negotiating a new union contract and wants everyone's birthday as a holiday every year, you, as a manager, may initially think that cannot be done. However, think of the trade-off. Maybe you will be willing to give them half-days at times they select. In this case, you have not given a full day but it's a half of a day that they can select. Two things have occurred here. First, you have not given them exactly what they asked for in the sense of a full day and that day being their birthday. The second thing is, however, that you have given them something and that is a half-day that can be selected by them. If they care to select their birthday, they can. The two positive things that have occurred here are that first, the union representative has accomplished something and has not "left the table" about this issue with a resounding "no" for an answer. He has obtained something for his people. The second thing is that you have retained a degree of control by selecting what you have given them and not adhering exactly with what was proposed to you by the other side.

So you see, if you have several issues varying in importance to you and if the other side has several issues varying in importance to them, you can give away or trade off on the smaller issues first. This shows that you are willing to negotiate and want to come about with some settlement, and you will find that this works wonders when you are negotiating.

Be Prepared to Walk Away

Being ready to walk away from a negotiation does not mean you should stomp out of a meeting in a huff! It does mean that you must always be ready to calmly get up from a chair and walk away, indicating that negotiations have not gelled. This is not recommended as a routine step and is appropriate only in certain cases. Representatives of nations in international negotiations have been known to snap their attaché cases closed, excuse themselves, and head for the airport. Coolly and calmly. This gave the other parties the opportunity to think about what the departure meant for the negotiations. Use this tactic only as a last resort.

If you are a potential home buyer and let your emotions rule by saying, "Great house!" you have left yourself no room to negotiate. If the seller or his agent is not willing to budge on the asking price, simply indicate that while you have the buying ability and are interested in purchasing the property, you are not ready to meet the seller's demand or make a counteroffer. You simply leave the negotiations. Unless your demands are outrageous, you will soon get an invitation to resume negotiations.

Compliments after Negotiations

Complimenting the other party is not only a courtesy; it sets the tone for subsequent meetings. This courtesy can be observed at any courthouse when a big case concludes. Although only one side won the case, the attorneys congratulate and compliment each other on good presentations. After a football game, the coaches congratulate each other even though only one won the game. Congratulating the opposing party is courteous and an essential part of the negotiating game.

Conclusion

Everyone on the planet is tuned to station WIIFM (What's in it for me?). WIIFM does not represent a selfish motivation. It is human nature to assess a situation and determine its potential benefit. In any business dealing, you should know your WIIFM and the WIIFM of the other side. This information will enable you to give and accept trade-offs and negotiate any issue successfully.

17

CURRENT CONCEPTS, TRENDS, AND TOOLS

This chapter discusses current trends and their pros and cons. They are not presented in any particular order. "Current" does not necessarily mean "new."

Working from Home (Telecommuting)

Telecommuting arrangements vary. Some people work from home one day a week; some work primarily from home and visit the office for certain meetings. Telecommuting must be considered from the view of the person who wants to work from home and the view of the employer that needs the work done. Whether the arrangement is productive depends on the type of work, the person, and the home environment. If you plan to work from home:

1. Set up an office with computer, printer, fax, scanner, and speaker phone. Do not attempt to work regularly from a laptop computer on a dining room table.
2. Be sure you have the personality to work from home. In an office, you have people to talk to during the day. If you work at home, you must be able to handle the quiet and isolation.
3. Exercise discipline. Don't visit the refrigerator frequently or leave the office "for a few minutes" to go to the bank or the dry cleaner. Take time for lunch and do errands then. Don't take time from work to have your car washed.
4. Provide a suitable home environment. Allowing distractions such as small children playing nearby is not conducive to serious work.
5. Provide a suitable environment for videoconferencing. Other conference participants (including your supervisor) don't want

to see evidence that you are cleaning house and "squeezing in" your employer's work.

6. Dress appropriately for work. You will feel more professional and this is essential when you are videoconferencing.

7. Understand the momentum of working in a home office. Don't let social calls and other interruptions interfere with that momentum.

If you follow these suggestions, you can probably work productively from a home office whether you work for a large firm or own a home-based business.

Social Responsibility

Social responsibility includes environmental considerations. This is not a new concept. Many large companies have been socially responsible for years. The concept involves awareness of a company's responsibility to its employees, customers, neighborhood, and the environment. It requires more than simple compliance with local, state, and federal regulations. It's about making conscious efforts to be fair to employees, provide quality products to consumers, participate in community affairs, and avoid contamination of the environment.

Many companies take their social responsibilities far beyond legal compliance. We'll discuss two of them* that share mutual concerns for consumers and the environment.

One is Johnson & Johnson, a pharmaceutical company. Its website, www.jnj.com, includes various links. One is *Our Caring* that provides sublinks such as *Environment, People, Access to Medicines*, and more.

The S C Johnson Company manufactures Edge, Windex, Glade, and other home products. Its www.scjohnson.com website homepage links to *Environment* and *Social Investment*. Many other companies exhibit social responsibilities in line with their products and profits.

No one can tell you exactly what activity constitutes socially responsible conduct or even define it for you. You do what you think best for your company and evaluate companies you deal with based on your own standards.

---

* Despite the name similarities, the companies are not related.

Domestic and Foreign Outsourcing

Outsourcing has become more common in recent years and it isn't going away soon. One reason is that many people will accept lesser quality for a lower price. Every company must decide whether outsourcing is suitable for its operation based on analysis of many factors.

Outsourcing can be domestic or offshore (foreign). A company can "contract out" segments of its manufacturing operation and produce a quality product.

Consider ABC Pharmaceuticals, a fictional drug manufacturer in New Jersey. ABC can conduct research and development at its own location, then manufacture, test, and package product at that same location. Alternatively, it can contract with DEF Company to order and mix chemicals for capsule production, then send the bulk mix to GHI Company for filling into capsules. GHI, in turn, sends the capsules in large containers of 500,000 or more capsules to JKL Packaging where they are filled into bottles of 5,000 each. The bottles are labeled appropriately and shipped to distributors that fill orders from pharmacies.

Why do companies outsource certain operations? Cost savings. How can companies benefit by making products offshore and then incur shipping costs from India or China, for example? Because the cost of shipping is far offset by the low cost of producing abroad. The economies of many countries allow low wages along with minimal regulation. Employees in such countries earn a fraction of what U.S. production employees earn. The amount varies with the product and location. In many cases, foreign workers are paid only one-half to one-twentieth of the wages earned by a comparable worker in the U.S. Why do the people work for such low wages? Because such wages represent good pay based on the economies of their countries.

Compliance with government regulations is expensive. Domestic labor regulations cover issues such as clean air and effluents, and safety standards for employees. Many countries do not impose stringent requirements on employers and therefore the employers incur lower costs. Is pollution an issue? Foreign governments are beginning to realize the impacts of pollution and may soon enact regulations, thus increasing production costs.

What about quality? Offshore production of pharmaceuticals must meet U.S. Food & Drug Administration (FDA) standards if the products are to be sold in the U.S. That means contractors for U.S. companies must comply with the FDA requirements and the U.S. company must monitor compliance. Items like clothing are not regulated so strictly and significant trade-offs in quality occur. Despite that, many consumers buy based on price.

Incidentally, if you wonder if there are additional costs incurred by U.S. citizens in contrast to savings, there are. In the pharmaceutical case given above, currently the Food and Drug Administration (FDA) is saying that it has "inadequate resources" to inspect every foreign firm that produces pharmaceutical intermediates or finished drug product for U.S. companies. They don't have to do that.

They have to inspect foreign firms that want to sell their pharmaceutical products in the United States. Regarding the foreign firms that are contractors of U.S. companies, those U.S. companies have the responsibility to inspect their contractors. So we have a case of a government agency doing the domestic company's work for them. If additional persons are hired to conduct all the inspections that are claimed to be needed, the U.S. taxpayers will be paying for a government regulatory agency to do the manufacturers' work for them.

Governments outsource work. In a March 2008 article in *The Washington Times*, Bill Gertz wrote, "The United States has outsourced the manufacturing of its electronic passports to overseas companies—including one in Thailand that was victimized by Chinese espionage—raising concerns that cost savings are being put ahead of national security, an investigation by *The Washington Times* has found."

Several states have purchased American flags from China. Various states have proposed legislation requiring that flags be purchased from U.S. manufacturers for patriotic reasons. Federal legislation now prohibits manufacturers from using "Made in the USA" labels unless the entire product was made in the U.S.

The primary objection to outsourcing is the elimination of jobs. If all U.S. citizens had satisfactory jobs, outsourcing would probably not encounter objections. Another problem is counterfeiting of electronics, sneakers, and other products—a Rolex watch costing $250 is certainly not a Rolex. Two very good books on overseas outsourcing are *Take This Job and Ship It* by Byron L. Dorgan, St. Martin's Press, 2006, and *Exporting America* by Lou Dobbs, Warner Business Books, 2004.

Not Invented Here (NIH) Syndrome

Don't confuse this NIH with the National Institutes of Health. NIH syndrome is not good for consumers. It is paradoxical that some companies that want to appear innovative only look inward and restrict themselves to their own activities (see Chapter 20). While some companies welcome ideas from outside inventors, others limit research and development (R & D) to their own facilities for a variety of reasons.

They may have NIH syndrome, based solely on ego—no one outside the company is as intelligent as in-house staff, and listening to an outsider's ideas would be a waste of valuable time even if the outsider owns patents on a product or procedure. In reality, if an outsider has the patent received or pending, then the large company simply has to look at applications of the product or process.

A company may want to entertain outside ideas but fears litigation. Companies have been sued for "stealing ideas" after they talked to inventors and realized they already had similar products or processes. Big companies have an advantage in being able to prove they already had a technology that is involved in litigation. However, the time, money, and aggravation required to defend such suits, as well as the unfavorable publicity, make them necessarily skittish about talking to outside inventors who may or may not be legitimate.

Companies that have R & D functions and also talk to inventors usually have a large number of ideas in progress by virtue of the philosophy of listening to others. They may not actively solicit ideas, but they will not exhibit NIH syndrome and will listen to you. You will be required to sign a Confidentiality Disclosure Agreement (CDA) or Confidentiality Agreement (CA) or Non Disclosure Agreement (NDA). These are different names for the same thing. It's O K, and preferred, to sign such an agreement. However, be sure that if there is an exclusivity clause in it indicating that you talk to no others while they are evaluating it such a clause has an expiration date beyond which you can show the invention to others. This precludes the company from letting your innovation sit while a competitor may come out with something similar to it.

Tools of Your Trade

Every business requires tools, whether the business is large or small, or involves production, science, engineering, or professional services. Such tools may be mechanical, personal, or administrative, for example:

Intellect—There are no substitutes for common sense and nerve. Trust in yourself. Know when you need information and know when you have enough information to act.

Accurate sources of information—Knowing when you have enough information to act is good practice, but you must also know the degree of accuracy of the information. Receiving information from a friend, business associate, boss, the Internet, or newspaper doesn't guarantee its truth or accuracy. Know the degree of reliability of your sources and rely only on the best.

Internet—This source enables you to obtain a wealth of knowledge almost instantly. Twenty years ago, information gathering entailed a visit to a library. Now you can, through Google and other search engines, find data in minutes. However, search engines help you find information; they do not verify it. Keep in mind the different degrees of reliability attributable to sources. A related caveat is to be very careful about what you put on a social networking site. Anything that portrays you in a negative light will be discovered and influence people who may be in a position to hire you or do business with you. Careers have been ruined by a single keystroke. Use the Internet for constructive activities.

E-mail—This is very useful for communicating instantaneously with individuals or large groups. Another caution is in order here. Whatever you write in an e-mail lives forever and can be accessed at any time. Be careful what you say and be cautious before hitting the "reply all" button. Sometimes only a sender needs an answer. At times, a telephone call is best. Don't use e-mail for convenience if you believe that a phone call is more appropriate. You might send an e-mail after business hours asking the best time to call the next day. Be sure to mention the subject. This step will prepare the recipient for your call.

Teleconferencing and videoconferencing—These are most useful for communicating with several persons at once about a common subject, getting immediate feedback and suggestions, and making joint decisions. If you are videoconferencing, make sure the background is non-distracting and that you dress properly.

Networking—This is a continuous activity conducted in person, by phone, and via the Internet. It involves making friends in your business world and knowing on whom you can rely for what. You will do favors for people in your network and they will reciprocate when necessary. The difference between politics and networking is that a politician will want a favor returned. A favor granted in the course of networking goes into a pool and the recipient passes it on by doing a favor for someone else.

Telephone—Old and true and still the best when you want to talk to someone and get immediate feedback to include their voice tones and inflections, things that an e-mail doesn't convey.

Meeting Face-to-Face—Whenever possible this is the best tool to convey information, judge reactions, and acquire information. Depending on the reliability of your interpretations, meeting remains the most accurate means of communication. This is why the best salespersons—those who work on commission only—meet and talk with their clients. They can see the clients' responses and react accordingly.

Contract Assignments and Short Term Employment

There are three classes of this type of work. The first is working temporarily for an employer. You perform a "regular" job, but you and your employer agree that the situation is temporary—until a person on leave returns, a department reorganizes, or a seasonal increase subsides. Another arrangement is working through a temporary employment agency. The agency hires you and assigns you to an employer as a "temp." You are paid by the agency which in turn is paid by the client company.

The other is if you are a consultant and work at different places, some of whom compete with each other. In this situation you may be sent there under contract to a large consulting organization or you may be there as an individual consultant. If the former, then your pay comes from the large consulting organization and if as an individual, you are paid directly by the client.

Here are some things to know about these classifications.

If you are a "temp" you may or may not have "benefits" such as health insurance. They may or may not work something out with you. If you are sent regularly to firms by an agency, that agency may provide benefits. It's worth checking with them.

As a consultant, you usually have to provide your own health insurance. You may be required to provide liability insurance. This varies with the type of consultant you are and therefore the nature of the projects on which you will be working.

If you are a "temp" you may have to pay your own taxes or the agency or client will take them out of your check for you. If they take out your various taxes they will, by the end of January of the following year, send you a W-2 form, which states what you earned and what they took out and sent to the state and federal governments for you. As a consultant you are paid your fee and are reimbursed for any expenses. However, you are responsible for sending your various taxes quarterly. The state and federal revenue agencies accept what you say quarterly, but for your annual filing they want proof. This proof is on your statements sent to you by your clients. These statements are 1099s. The 1099 is the form on which they make the statement of your earnings. Sometimes you will hear a person ask another person "Are you a W-2 or a 1099?" which is a slang way of asking them if their client withheld their taxes or not.

Here's a very important aspect of doing contract work. In addition to doing a good job because you have high ethics and work standards, you will be expected to maintain confidentiality. You may be handling the company's top secret documents. You may also have access to employees' personal data. You consultants already know this. For you "temps" who know this, fine. For those of you for whom this is a reminder, take heed. You are not likely to deliberately talk about the proprietary issues or products of a client company. No, not normally. However don't let yourself slip when being interviewed by a potential new client who says "Tell me about other projects on which you've worked." Think! There are some things, a little bit general, that you can say. There are things, specific to a previous client's confidential projects that you cannot say. This is very important. Being competent is one aspect of you as a potential contractor; being able to "keep your mouth shut" is as valuable.

Bonuses

A bonus should be a generous reward for extra good work. Bonuses should never be publicized or anticipated. After you promise a bonus to an employee, he will direct his efforts to gaining the bonus and possibly exclude important activities that do not contribute to this bonus.

The bonus system is usually counterproductive and usually applies to a limited group. For example, sales bonuses usually reward exceptional sales; plant managers may receive bonuses for exceeding production. Before you decide to implement bonuses, ask yourself whether the level of activity required for a bonus adequately determines superior performance that benefits the company. Consider the following:

Example 1—A plant manager receives a bonus for the amount of product shipped and not for its quality. A significant amount of inferior product is shipped and recorded. Customers are dissatisfied, but the plant manager receives the bonus.

Example 2—A salesperson receives a bonus for making a large number of phone calls in a day although no sales are made because the potential customers have not been given the opportunity to ask questions.

Example 3—A CEO receives a bonus because the company stock price rises to a certain figure. The bonus involves direct payment and additional shares of company stock. The CEO directs his efforts to increasing the stock price at the expense of long-term projects such as the purchase of new equipment that will increase the future value of the firm. (There have been CEOs of large companies who have caused their companies to lose billions of dollars and then they received bonuses of millions of dollars for that! Some were retained and some were let go. They all got their bonuses. How can a company justify bonuses or severance packages of millions of dollars to executives who performed badly? The answer is in the wording of the bonus statement.)

Awards

We all need recognition to a degree. Some people need only a smile, while others want salary increases. Still others need a more visible form of recognition, such as a plaque or an announcement at a meeting. Hollywood grants awards all the time and recipients immediately increase salary demands for their next movies.

In Chapter 16, we cautioned readers to not only listen to what people *say*, but be aware of what they *don't say*. A similar situation applies here. Look beyond the good feeling enjoyed by the winner and consider the (possibly) negative feelings of those who did not receive awards but thought they should have. Presenting an award may produce more harm than good. Consider the impact on other good performers when you decide to give a person or group an award. If you want to recognize extraordinary performance, present generous bonuses as a surprise to deserving persons or groups.

Here's a question without an answer or comment. Did you ever notice that the alumni who donate the most money to the university get the largest award for being the "Person of The Year?" Did you see that it's given at a banquet in their honor?

Here's another question without an answer or comment. Did you ever notice that organizations such as Chambers of Commerce and others send out solicitations for names of potential awards recipients at their annual awards banquet? Maybe that time would be better spent networking.

Attempts to Mislead

People will deliberately mislead you at times. In fact, they will outright lie to you. We sometimes give reflex answers that indicate approval of feeble excuses. When you see some of these in print you'll see how weak they are. Let people who try to mislead you know that you're aware of the attempt. Table 17.1 shows a number of incorrect or insincere statements, their true meanings, and suggested responses and relevant comments.

Accuracy of Information

People sometimes pass on erroneous information they think is correct. This is different from a deliberate lie. You must know how to assess the accuracy of information. Here are some tips:

1. Know your source. You should know the credibility of people you supervise, associate with, and socialize with and how accurate their information is.
2. Be objective. Don't assume that if the information is what you want to hear, it must be correct.
3. Verify information whenever possible.
4. Never assume that information from a newspaper or the Internet must be correct.
5. Be aware that information you receive may be incomplete or repeated out of context.

Let's review an example. A town wanted an appropriation for a new playground. The town council agreed to an amount and a county official turned it down. When the newspaper printed news of the refusal, the residents became angry at the county official. At the next meeting, the town council, at the urging of the politician, appropriated a much larger amount for a bigger playground and sports complex. The county official declined the initial offering because he knew the sum was insufficient to build the required facility. His action led to a larger appropriation for a better facility, despite the initial negative public reaction. The point is that you must know all the facts before you pass judgment. Get all the facts, assess your sources, determine the accuracy of the facts, and look at all sides of an issue before making a judgment.

Table 17.1 What People Say and What They Mean

WHAT PEOPLE SAY OR DO	WHAT THEY REALLY MEAN BUT DON'T SAY	COMMENTS
I've been busy, very busy, so busy. I didn't get to return your call.	Everything I've been doing for the last several days has been more important than returning your call.	Reply - Oh! I wanted to give you…money, business, an account, information…but that's O K. I gave it to someone else (especially if that someone else is a competitor outside or within the company).
Let's wait 15 more minutes for the latecomers (for a meeting) to show up.	I am only a figurehead, and am insecure. I don't want to offend anyone so we should wait. Wasting the time of those of you who are here on time isn't as important as me being a nice person.	That's insulting, and it's wasting the time of those who were on time.
Apply a "surcharge" to a bill.	We're greedy and you're dumb so we're taking advantage of that combination by taking more of your money without raising prices to fool you into paying us more.	You say - "You're greedy but I'm not dumb. You got your surcharge today but you have now lost my business and that of the 10 people I am going to tell."
Display a sign that says "Not Responsible for…."	If we shirk our duty we don't want you to sue us, so we hope you believe this sign.	You say - "Some things you are not responsible for and some things you are responsible for. I, and my lawyer, will determine which is which."
Attach a note to an e-mail, "If you have received this by mistake you are obligated to return it or dispose of it and tell us…."	We may have erroneously sent this to you. It's our fault but we want to coerce you into thinking you have an obligation to us.	You are entitled to keep and dispose of anything anyone sends you unsolicited. You say, "I may return it or dispose of it out of courtesy but not if you lie to me and tell me I am obligated to correct your errors."
During a holding period on voicemail, "This call may be monitored for Quality Control Purposes."	We want you to think we have quality control…that we care about you. You may even be fool enough to believe it.	If they cared and had any quality control, they wouldn't have placed you on hold for so long.

(*continued*)

Table 17.1 What People Say and What They Mean (continued)

WHAT PEOPLE SAY OR DO	WHAT THEY REALLY MEAN BUT DON'T SAY	COMMENTS
We're going to "launch an _____ initiative." (Between "an" and "initiative" a project name is filled in. For example, a "Quality initiative.")	This will look good on our project list and will keep us occupied while at work. We can meet periodically and talk about this. There are, of course, no goals or time frames set for completion.	The word "initiative" really means - The power or ability to begin or to follow through energetically with a plan or task; enterprise and determination. That doesn't count here. You mean you will start to discuss a project and then forget about it.
"The Market's bad" or "The economy's very low."	We fouled up but can't admit it. We made an inferior product, erroneous market projection, etc. We'll blame the market or the economy.	If you fouled up, at least be honest and take responsibility for your own actions.
All of our representatives are serving other customers. Please hold for the next available representative."	He's out to lunch...or asleep...or lost.	You cheapskates. Hire more help or I'll take my business somewhere else.
"...how you can help..."	We want your money	You may want to volunteer your time or knowledge, but these organizations only want your money. Where does the money go?
"For your convenience" we will automatically bill your credit card periodically. Simply sign and return the card.	"Not for your convenience; for our convenience. Now we have you on a hook. If you try to change this you may find it a bit difficult."	I'm not going to fall for that line. Next you'll tell me you have the Brooklyn Bridge for sale and will give me a special deal.

Note 1: There are blank spaces above for you to fill in some of the insincere things that you have observed. As you think of them, write them in and you'll know how to handle them in the future.

Note 2: In the first example it is important to remember that the people who never have time to return your calls or e-mails somehow always have time to ask for a favor. That tells you their priorities. Avoid these people if you can. They are at best inefficient and at worst parasitic.

PART IV
PLANNING AHEAD

18
Your Career

This chapter will assume you are employed by a medium to large company, although the principles still apply if you work for a very small company or hold what you regard as an interim job. You may be starting your career or you may be well into your career. The same principles apply. If you are at the start of your career, you may lack experience but you still have knowledge and talent. You may be searching for a new job within your company or elsewhere.

First, ask yourself certain fundamental questions, the answers to which will indicate what type of job you want. You don't have to answer yes or no. Your answer may be "some of each," in which case define the amounts of each. The questions have no right or wrong answers.

1. Do you like working indoors or outdoors?
2. Do you like interacting with other people or working in isolation?
3. Do you need credit (recognition, accolades, etc.) for doing a good job?
4. Do you need your credit for a good job to be seen by others?
5. Do you want to travel or not travel in the course of your work?
6. Do you want to see the results of your work applied or are you content to contribute a small part to a large project that may not reveal your efforts?
7. Do you want to manage people or simply work alone?
8. Do you want to manage projects or simply carry out assignments?
9. Do you want to work on single or multiple projects?
10. Do you want to address audiences or be a member of an audience?

These questions are intended to help you focus on what you want and find a position that fits your needs. People sometimes start down one career path and then change direction because a new opportunity appears. Restlessness may set in because you are so busy with your career you haven't had time to consider whether your present job is still really what you want. That's when to pause and ask yourself if you are satisfied. You may work for a good company and have a good boss but not necessarily be doing what you want. Your interests may change and trigger a desire to change career paths. You may decide to teach rather than work in industry or vice versa. Maybe you want to start your own business after a career in industry. You may have any number of reasons to leave your present position and do something else within or outside your company.

Your General Plan

Every career needs a plan. If you don't know where you're going, how will you know if you arrived? The answers to the 10 questions above should indicate what you want from a job. The next step is to look at where you want to be in 3, 5, or 10 years.

When you do that, you can then figure out how to get there. Once you know where you're going, you can draw your map. At this point in our discussion you can determine a sequence of events such as (using a laboratory as an example):

- I want to be the vice president (VP) of quality control (QC).
- I am currently an analyst and have a good record of conducting routine analyses.
- I want to develop new analytical methods as soon as possible.
- I plan to be promoted to section leader and supervise three other chemists within four years.
- I want to be the director of the laboratory within four years after that.
- I want to be promoted to VP of QC after three to five years of doing a very good job of directing the laboratory.

Certainly a lot of changes can occur in a company within a 10- to 12-year span. Laboratories can be consolidated, the company can relocate, or it may be acquired by another company. It is possible that someone not even employed by your company can be hired as the VP of QC while you are climbing the ladder. None of these potential events should prevent you from constructing your plan. Plans are made to be reviewed and modified along the path to completion.

You buy a ticket to a baseball or football game in an open stadium weeks in advance of the game, knowing it may rain on the day of the game. You plan a vacation in advance, not knowing if some unforeseen event may disrupt your plan and derail your vacation. We all make plans based on current conditions and best guesses about possible obstacles. You must believe in your ability to surmount any obstacles in your path or change your path and still find satisfaction in your life and your career. You may have to modify your plan, but that isn't a valid reason not to plan. Planning is essential. Executives don't reach those levels in companies just because they happen to work there. They had plans and pursued alternatives when the original plans didn't work out and the end results may have been better than planned.

Your Strategic Plan

Chapter 14 covered strategic plans in a company context. We will now repeat the five fundamental steps of planning that also apply to your career:

- Decide where you want to go.
- Determine what is required to get there.
- Make the decision.
- Implement the decision.
- Monitor feedback.

This is an appropriate point to review the WOTS UP (weaknesses, opportunities, threats, and strengths underlying planning) analysis also covered in Chapter 14. The point here is that the same strategic planning process used by companies can be applied to your own career goals. Use the principles shown in Chapter 14 to construct your own strategic plan, review it periodically, and modify it to accommodate changes that have occurred.

Meet New People

Meeting new people at work leads to knowing more about the company and having more people know who you are. Instead of going to lunch with the same group every day, resolve to have lunch with a new person you want to know. If you do that every two weeks, you will meet 25 new people in a year. Invite the person to lunch a few days in advance. You won't meet new people and learn about other operations if you lunch with the same people every day.

If you are in a company of 30,000 employees and you are in a new entry level position, don't try to have lunch with the CEO immediately. Have lunch with peers in other areas or employees one level higher. If you're a laboratory analyst, look for a section supervisor, salesperson, or financial analyst.

The reason for meeting at lunch is because it doesn't interfere with your work or anyone else's. Ask to meet at lunch personally or by phone, not by e-mail. Simply say you heard of the person and want to learn about his work. When you have lunch, ask the person how he reached his current position; for example, "What made you select marketing as a profession?" or "You manage a group. What exactly are your responsibilities?" Listen to the answer. Don't interrupt. And don't talk about yourself unless you are asked a question.

If you listen to this person, you will learn and also give the gift of listening that 90% or more of the people they interact with daily do not give them. Listening works wonders.

Observe

You can learn about people by watching them—not staring at them. If you are watching someone at a high level make a presentation, watch him or her carefully. That person will dress appropriately, look confident, be prepared with notes and visual aids, and be ready to respond to questions. Listen to the delivery of the presentation, both for content and the style of delivery. Yogi Berra, a Hall of Fame baseball player, in *Berra's Law,* wrote "You can observe a lot just by watching." Berra played for the New York Yankees as a catcher, then managed the Yankees and later the New York Mets. Look at people you want to emulate and learn from them. Look at people who you want to be like and do what they do. Look at people who you don't want to be like and don't do what they do.

Visibility

Be sure that you have a good boss. If you do not respect the person to whom you report, transfer somewhere else where you do have a good boss. The next step is to achieve visibility. Let's continue with our example of a laboratory analyst.

If you are an analyst, you can build a good record conducting analyses and you will have enjoyment and satisfaction at the same time. As your career progresses, however, it's helpful to be visible to others inside and outside the company. One way to accomplish this is to write a journal article, make a presentation at a professional meeting, or do both—present a published article you wrote at a professional meeting, with the blessings of your company and your boss, of course.

Another way to achieve visibility is to accompany a salesperson on a customer visit. You may get an opportunity to assist a customer with a technical problem. Sales productivity is measured directly by the sales generated. Salespersons are very visible and your assistance will be noted by people inside and outside your company.

Assisting manufacturing by designing new test procedures to ensure product quality will establish a good relationship with that area. Writing in-house reports and making presentations are other good ways to be noticed.

Job Descriptions

Human resources operations of large companies maintain written descriptions for every job, from executives to production workers. Job descriptions in small companies may not be as structured, but they will exist. When you were hired you were fitted into a particular job description. The job description is a reference for measuring your work. Your human resources department or supervisor can provide you with a copy. Sometimes employees want to review their job descriptions to determine whether they are doing more work than assigned in an effort to seek more pay. That doesn't go over well because bosses expect to be trusted. When you request your job description, say that you want it to learn more about what is expected of you.

Job description formats follow a general theme in both large and small companies. They usually cover:

- Position
- Title
- Department or Division
- Reports to (title of supervisor)
- Responsibilities (what is expected)
- Qualifications (education, work experience, and knowledge required; may include willingness to travel and proven leadership ability)

Optional categories such as working conditions may be included for specific jobs. The primary areas of concern for career planning are responsibilities and qualifications.

In discussions with your boss about your future, he may say, "I think you should move upward but I don't have a job description for the position." Be aware that he can work with human resources to develop one. If you know how your company's job descriptions are written, prepare one and give a copy to your boss. Simply say, "I know you're busy, but since you agree that I am qualified to move up and don't have the time to write a new job description, I have written it for you. Add, delete, or modify as you see fit, of course. If you have changes, I'll incorporate them for you." If you want to pursue a better job in your area, be sure that you have already taken on the responsibilities of the job. The best way to show that you can handle a higher position is to be already doing it.

Systems

Life is full of systems. Learn the systems you need to succeed. Do not fight the systems because they are designed to allow for the flow of knowledge, work, products, and employees from one area to another. Every company constitutes a large system containing several smaller systems. The hiring process is an example of a system. The process of scheduling employees to start and finish work is a system. Each industry has its own set of systems; companies may follow them and add their own as required. Governments have systems; so do households.

For the most part, you work within established systems that ensure that operations run efficiently. Changes are made when a system no longer functions effectively or when new technology can make it run better. You may be charged with inventing a new system or modifying an existing one, so learn to work within systems. The executives at the top learned to work within the company's systems. Mastering systems is a necessary step toward the top.

Interviews

You will be interviewed many times in your career—when seeking your first job, when applying for a promotion, and when looking for a job at another company. Keep some important points in mind:

1. Before an interview with a prospective employer, learn about the company, its products, and its philosophies by obtaining a copy of its annual report. Most annual reports of public companies are now available through their websites. Review the chairman's statement. This states the primary philosophies of the company. After that, get familiar with the products and in what areas the company wants to expand.
2. Be prepared to say how you can contribute to the company's success. Don't ask what the company has to offer. The company wants to know how you can help it achieve the goals stated in its annual report. Never drop names of people you know in the company. The name you drop may belong to a person who may be on the way out and this could ruin your chances.
3. Practice interviewing with a relative or friend. This will prepare you to answer questions clearly and concisely. Reverse the process and interview your relative or friend. This enlightening exercise will enable you to see the situation from the company view. Try it the next time you anticipate an interview.

What if a potential employer is not a publicly traded company and does not publish an annual report? You can acquire much information through public relations and advertising materials, with the exception of financial statements.

Other Considerations

Career planning involves other considerations such as working for a large or small company, relocating or staying in the same location, seeking promotion, or leaving a company. Here are some points to consider related to advantages and disadvantages:

Working for a large or small company—In a small company you are known to the management and may have varied duties. Your career can grow with the company. You can progress to top management if the company prospers. However, if the company falters or is sold, you may find yourself starting over. If you are with a new, small company and one of the two undesired events mentioned above occurs, it will occur after only a couple of years and you will not have invested half of your career there. In a large company, the path to the top is longer but the rewards are greater.

Relocating or remaining at one location—Generally, geographic moves are associated with promotions and rapid advancement in a large company. They usually involve increased responsibilities and salary. On the other hand, remaining at one location allows you and your family to be established in a community, and you can still pursue promotions that will result in a satisfying career.

Stay with one company or change companies—Remaining with one company will yield a good pension and interesting work. However, even old established companies can be sold and lead to management changes. Changing companies generally leads to promotion but may require relocation.

Final Words

If you have learned some career moving options presented above and you apply some of them to change a career that was not moving as fast as you planned, as they materialize you may feel like you had been driving with the parking brake on. When you realize the reason that the car—or your career—was not moving as fast as you wanted it to, and then you release the brake, you'll have a wonderful feeling that you will get to your next career destination faster

19

STARTING YOUR OWN BUSINESS

First Steps

Most people will advise you to start a business by planning financing or researching taxes. These are important but not the first tasks to be done. Before you deal with these issues, you must address the following issues:

1. Know your product or service. Ask yourself, "What business am I in?" The answer requires a degree of specificity. (In a large corporation, the board of directors should ask this question at every quarterly meeting.)
2. Know your customers or clients.

You cannot determine your needs for money, work space, or time to launch your business until you answer these questions accurately. Clearly defining your business means asking more questions:

- What is the nature of your business? Be specific.
- Who are your customers or clients?
- Where are your customers or clients?
- Why should they buy your product or service?
- Why should they buy it from you?

If you don't have customers, you don't have a business!

Unique Selling Proposition (USP)

A unique selling proposition distinguishes your business from businesses of competitors. Your USP is also your "area of distinctive competence." Put yourself in the position of your customer. Would you buy from your company? Why or why not? To determine how to set your business apart:

- Define your USP.
- List factors that make your business stand above the competition.
- List advantages your business can provide (and your competitors can't).

Customers look at three factors when they choose a product of service: price, quality, and speed (see Figure 19.1). We covered these factors in Chapter 8.

You will go out of business if you attempt to achieve being the best in all three.

Construct a Strategic Plan to include what you want to do with your business...whether you intend to build it, or build it and sell it. The elements of the Strategic Plan were discussed in Chapter 14 and I refer you to that with the recommendation that you do this for your own business. If you are an individual starting your own business your plan need only be a couple of pages. It's possible to get so engrossed in the planning that you don't get to the actual starting of the business. You don't need a hundred pages at this time. You need a clear picture of what you want to do and how you are going to do it. That can be said in a few paragraphs. There's a time for planning and a time for action.

Price-Quality-Speed
Select any two

Figure 19.1   Select any two.

Know that only about 50% of what people tell you is true. The untrue part is composed of both deliberate lies and, more often, people telling you what they think is true. Verify information. Know which are the accurate sources and which are not...that's people, websites, news media, relatives, friends, associates, etc. (this was addressed in Chapter 17, Current Concepts, Trends and Tools).

Partners: Pros and Cons

Have you considered starting a business with one or more partners? Do you need them? If they have some talent needed for your business (and you don't have it), think about a partnership. However, every participant in a team or partnership must "bring something to the table" such as expertise or financing. Without participation, you don't need a partner.

If you decide to pursue a partnership, determine the degree of partnership participation with regard to financing, decision making, and effort; then engage an attorney to prepare a partnership agreement covering these points and any other legal issues. Partnerships fail when partners can't agree on purchases, services or products, customers, and other issues, or when one partner does not carry his share of the responsibilities.

Beware of anyone who wants you to put up the money and he will put in "sweat equity" and "knowledge." You are taking all the risks and they are taking none.

Beware of involving relatives in the business. Having similar DNA only goes so far. It doesn't mean you and a blood relative have the same personalities, work ethic, risk taking characteristics, energy, and so on.

Beware of anyone who, in your opinion, is not carrying his/her share of the work, finance, and responsibility. They are simply taking from you and giving nothing in return.

Know how to recognize when people lack integrity and don't deal with them. Learn the early indications of people's lack of integrity.

Let's look at the case where someone else is starting a business and wants you to be a partner. Beware of anyone who wants you to do the work and instead of paying you money wants to give you "stock options". They want you to work for them for nothing. They want your knowledge, expertise, and contacts. (Yes indeed - contacts - they want you to introduce them to your friends, who after they have been fleeced by this "partner" will no longer be your friends.) If their company fails you have options on nothing and they have all your contacts.

People with whom you do business should have the following characteristics:

1. Look you in the eye and shake hands with you.
2. Pay promptly.
3. Should not start conversations by saying that "...things are tough and the budget is tight..." with their department or company. (They're going to try to get a discount for no real reason other than they are cheap. If you give it to them they won't pay on time anyway.)
4. Should not start conversations by saying that the nation's economy is slow. (They're going to try to get a discount for no real reason other than they are cheap. If you give it to them they won't pay on time anyway.) That's the same parenthetical comment as in Number 3 above.

Customer Issues

Your customers should also follow certain ethical practices. A customer should look you in the eye, shake your hand, not complain about tough economies and tight budgets and, most importantly, pay promptly. For more information about working with customers, see Chapter 16.

Your customers will also expect certain behavior from you. Don't "nickel and dime" your customers. What would you think if a restaurant charged you for sugar, mustard, or water? Such practices drive customers to competitors. You should allow yourself a fair margin on your product or service and thus not have to implement small charges that annoy customers. A business can fail by charging the lowest prices to undercut competition. An inadequate margin means that a slight adversity like a late payment can start a business on the road to financial problems.

View your business from your customer's view. Call your business to assess the treatment your customers receive. If you have a website and "contact us" link, try it. Measure the time required to get a response and check other parameters of the site. Ask a friend to visit your business as a customer and make a purchase to evaluate customer treatment. Contact the customer service department. Experiencing customer treatment is the best way to check performance—better than accounting evaluations, marketing surveys, and blaming the economy. Viewing your business as your customer sees it allows you to diagnose problems effectively and solve them quickly.

Financing and Credit

Don't borrow money to start a business unless you have no choice. Never use credit cards to finance a business! They can legally charge up to 30% interest.* Trying to repay large credit card debts can require energy you should devote to building your business and customer base.

You may occasionally need credit in the start-up of your business. Establish a relationship with your bank and get to know the bank manager personally. A good relationship with your bank will benefit both of you.

Ask the bank to establish a line of credit for use as needed instead of seeking a loan. This will enable you to borrow smaller amounts and pay less interest than you would on a large lump-sum loan. For example, a $100,000 line of credit means that amount is available to you. If you need $25,000, you can withdraw that amount and retain an available balance of $75,000; and you will pay interest only on the $25,000 used.

Don't deal with lenders who base decisions only on a credit report. Credit reports can be erroneous because reporting companies acquire information from various sources and do not verify its accuracy. Deal only with lenders who talk with you and fairly evaluate your ability to repay a debt. Consider the quality of the lender along with interest rate. Sometimes a lender whose rate is a bit higher (a tenth of a point)

---

* Most credit card companies are incorporated in Delaware or North Dakota because those states have no usury laws, impose no limits on interest rates, and their laws (not the laws of the state where a borrower resides) apply to credit disputes. Furthermore, most credit card companies can legally change interest rates at will without notice.

may be more understanding if you have a temporary problem and will assist you in working out a new schedule of payments. This is a situation in which it's beneficial to know the bank manager. Never make late payments or skip payments; communicate with the lender and work with him to resolve the problem.

Lenders can assist you by providing different types of business financing such as term loans and revolving lines of credit (discussed above). In addition to these traditional forms of financing, you may want to investigate whether equity financing (or venture capital) is a viable option for obtaining business capital. Learn about various credit products and choose one that suits your needs. For more information on different loan products, contact your local lender or visit the Small Business Administration's website at www.sba.gov.

20

... And A Little Bit More

I hope that the contents of this book will help you as you go through your career and as you travel through life. Whether you are beginning your career, advancing through various levels of management, work as a senior executive, or are planning your retirement, I hope you will have found the material in this book helpful. This last chapter presents a montage of anecdotes on various subjects and bits of wisdom in no particular order.

Expectations

You don't always get what you want but invariably you will get what you expect!

Ask National Football League coaches or coaches of various sports, both professional and college. They will tell you that everybody wants to win. Who's going to tell you they want to lose or they don't care to win? Those that win routinely are those that have prepared themselves properly and actually expect to win.

Remember, if you want to avoid disappointments in life, then simply don't expect anything because anything you're ever disappointed about is an expectation that did not come to fruition. Therefore, if you don't expect anything, and don't plan anything, you should never be disappointed. That's how some people think! That's not you and me! We plan and we practice and rehearse and we expect to accomplish our goals.

The five steps in planning are:

- Where do you want to go?
- What does it take to get there?
- Make the decision.
- Implement (do it).
- Monitor, Feedback.

Professional Characteristics

Professionals in every field exhibit certain common traits that clearly distinguish them from inconsistent performers. A professional:

- Is honest
- Performs consistently
- Is always prepared
- Is always on time
- Uses all available resources and never wastes time or energy on nonproductive activities
- Accepts responsibility; never makes excuses
- Concentrates on the goal; focuses on the task to be achieved
- Is organized
- Is knowledgeable
- Is objective despite personal views
- Is decisive; has courage to make decisions
- Is self-assured
- Communicates well

Risk

The following observation says more about risk than a long explanation.*

> To laugh is to risk appearing the fool.
> To weep is to risk appearing sentimental.
> To reach out for another is to risk involvement.
> To expose feelings is to risk exposing your true self.
> To place your ideas, your dreams before the crowd is to
>   risk loss.
> To love is to risk not being loved in return.
> To live is to risk dying.
> To hope is to risk despair.
> To try at all is to risk failure.
> But risk we must.
> Because the greatest hazard of life is to risk nothing.

---

* I saw this material many years ago and cannot recall the source.

Profit Improvement: Back to Basics*

Business is an art as well as a science and a matter of practical experience, judgment, foresight, and luck. To be successful in business, we must never forget the basics.

1. The role of business in a free society is to organize and coordinate the factors of production to produce the goods and services that people want at prices they are willing and able to pay.
2. The wants, needs, and desires of your customers determine and direct business activity. If you satisfy your customers, you will grow and prosper. [*Corollary: If your company is not growing and prospering, it is because you are not satisfying your customers in sufficient quantity, for whatever reason.*]
3. Customers always want the very most for the very least. In this, they are selfish, demanding, ruthless, and disloyal. They will abandon a supplier or vendor whenever they feel they can be served better elsewhere. Customers always make rational decisions, i.e., they are always right. They patronize those individuals and businesses that serve them the best. [*Corollary: In a dynamic market, there are always opportunities for those who can find new, better, faster, cheaper ways to serve customers with what they want.*]
4. As long as there are customer needs unmet or better or cheaper ways to meet them, there are money-making opportunities for you.
5. There are always business opportunities if you are willing to (a) lower your demands (prices or wages); (b) restructure your offerings (new products or services); (c) change your customers.
6. The purpose of your business is to create customers. Profits are the results of creating enough customers and serving them satisfactorily at prices above total costs of production and distribution.
7. It is not what producers produce but what customers prefer that determines economic activity and economic rewards.

---

* This very helpful material is from a lecture by Ned Frey, a business trainer.

[*Corollaries: Customers, not corporations, pay all wages. Everyone has at least one customer.*]

8. The key to business success has always been finding a need and filling it.

9. Your success will always be determined by (a) what you do; (b) demands for your product or service; (c) the difficulty of replacing you.

10. If you want more profits, you must concentrate on increasing the value of your service. The focus on outward contribution is the hallmark of effective men and women.

11. The market pays superior rewards only for superior goods and services and average rewards for average goods and services. Business success comes from developing excellence in a particular market-related area.

12. Successful people make a habit of doing what failures don't like to do. The master key to riches is self-discipline: doing what is necessary to achieve your goals.

Setbacks

Every career encounters setbacks. A setback can last a day (a key person fails to appear for a meeting) or far longer (a problem boss). Look upon these and other setbacks as potholes on a road. You may hit it and damage a tire, stop your car and attempt to repair the hole, or swing around it. Obviously the third alternative is preferred because it allows you to continue to your destination and is applicable to obstacles in your career path. Swing around them instead of stopping and wasting time on them.

Attitude

As you move through you career and through life, you will find that where some people look at situations as problems, others look at them as opportunities. Much of what you get out of your career and out of life is THE WAY YOU LOOK AT THINGS! When you first became a manager, you had to look at things differently than when you first started your working career. If you had continued looking at things exactly the same way as when you started your career, you would not have progressed. It was learning how to look at things in this different manner and then subsequently learning again how to look at things as promotions came along that helped you. In fact, adjusting the way you looked at things before the promotion was in a large part responsible for the promotion. Please keep that in mind. It has helped you in the past and it will continue to help you. And if you are saying to yourself that this is simply a description of your attitude, you're absolutely correct. It's all about having the proper attitude.

Time—Your Nonrenewable Resource

We are well aware that we should not waste valuable resources. Everywhere we look we see slogans and other reminders that we should save our valuable resources. We should not waste water, energy, paper products, and more.

That leads us to ask ourselves what we mean by "resources." This is an important, yet sometimes non-defined, term. Companies and departments within those companies say that they have "inadequate resources" to accomplish a project. They say they "need more resources."

If you want more resources, you should be more specific regarding what it is you need. Ask for the specific resources and you may get them. Be vague and you may not get them.

Resources can be:

Money
Buildings
Personnel
Equipment
Information
Your own intellect
Time
And any more you think about

You often have the proper resource and are not utilizing it properly. Let's look at, for example, personnel. Before you say you need more persons, look to see if those you have are doing what is most productive. Have you assigned them tasks that are directed to the goal of your company or department or have you assigned tangential tasks?

In my experience I have seen departments where 20% of the work being done was not needed. When the people were redirected to their proper goals, it was like having new people on board. Actually, the people felt better about the new assignments; they felt more productive, and they were more productive.

The first thing you do before asking for a new resource is to make sure you are using the existing one properly, that is, with no waste. Said another way, before you acquire any new resource, make sure you are not wasting the one you have.

Why is it, then, that so many people waste "time" on tangents, thereby straying from their primary goals? Before inadvertently traveling down tangent lane, be sure to keep your eye on your time and your goal.

Aside from your intellect and your ethics, your time is your most precious commodity.

It is unique in that we all have time assigned to be on this planet, and while our allotted times are different we all spend time at the same rate. Knowing this, isn't it worthwhile to be sure we are spending it wisely? Look to be sure that you are not wasting your time, and then plan the best way to spend it.

You will meet people who don't know the value of time. They get onto tangents routinely and because of this they don't accomplish what they set out to accomplish. At the end of the day they wonder why they didn't get much done. Since they have no respect for the value of their time they cannot have any respect for the value of your time. They will get onto tangents when talking to you and it's up to you to keep them on track. Deal with these people only when you must, and even then, be aware of their inadequacy in the time management area.

As you periodically check to ensure that you are not wasting energy, water, or any of a number of valuable resources, be sure to also check to ensure that you are not wasting your time—your nonrenewable resource.

Problem Solving

In order to solve a problem you must first identify it. Describe it in detail. Be specific.

Let's start with an example of problem solving by describing an actual problem that occurred and how it was solved. The item was a quantity of rubber stoppers for pharmaceutical use. They would be used on bottles for intravenous medication or on vials for use in injections.

The stoppers were black. The pharmaceutical manufacturer processed them by washing and sterilizing thousands of stoppers at the same time. After steam sterilization, white particles were observed on the stoppers. Since the stoppers were black it was easy to see the white particles, even though the particles were very small.

The pharmaceutical company was ready to return the stoppers to the stopper manufacturer in the belief that the white particles were, upon steam sterilization, coming out of the stoppers. Such an action would also delay the manufacturer of the pharmaceutical products since there was only a limited supply of stoppers in their inventory.

Before returning all 200,000 of them, it was agreed that the company would talk to the stopper manufacturer's sales representative and technical director on a conference call. On the pharmaceutical company side of this conference call were the production supervisor, the purchasing agent, and the director of manufacturing.

We'll skip all the details of the conversation and go directly to the solution. It turned out that, before sterilizing the stoppers, the pharmaceutical company's manufacturing supervisor covered them with kraft paper—the brown paper that is used as a durable wrapping paper. This was done so that the stoppers could be layered with a thousand or more spread flat on a large pan, covered with a sheet of kraft paper, then covered with another layer of stoppers and another sheet of paper and so on, until there were ten layers.

Upon further discussion it was revealed that the production supervisor was trying a new brand of kraft paper. After the introduction of the new kraft paper, the white particles began appearing. The plot thickened when the supervisor said that there were three production lines in the plant and that the new paper was used on only one of the lines. That was the one on which the particles appeared. The white particles were not appearing on the other lines. When asked why he was using a new brand of paper on the one line, he said that it was cheaper and that if it worked he would use it on all the lines.

There is a chemical, aluminum sulfate, used in the manufacture of this type of paper and it is known that the white crystals of the aluminum sulfate could come out of the paper under such conditions. Analysis of the white particles proved them to be aluminum sulfate.

The problem was solved, with some embarrassment on the faces of the pharmaceutical people who didn't identify it correctly in the first place.

Here's how the problem was originally stated:

White particles are appearing on the surfaces of the black stoppers upon steam sterilization. Since we (the pharmaceutical manufacturer) are not doing anything different, the stoppers must be at fault. (The company people, until the conference call, didn't think that using cheaper paper was "anything different.")

Here's how, after getting more information, the problem was restated:

White particles are appearing on the surfaces of the black stoppers upon steam sterilization. This occurs on line one, the line where we are using the new, cheaper kraft paper. It started the same time that we used the new paper. There is no problem on the other two lines where we have made no change.

Analysis was conducted to be sure not to jump to conclusions. Do you see how the more specific identification and definition of the problem made the solution more evident?

So you see, once the problem is identified more specifically, the solution is more readily apparent.

Here are some other considerations in the problem solving area:

- Determine whether you are part of the solution or part of the problem.
- Don't criticize the opposition.
- Don't tout your past record.
- Don't waste time saying "I told you so."
- Realize that determing blame is not a priority.
- Solve the problem at hand.
- Identify the problem in detail.
- Determine information needed to solve the problem.
- Decide how to obtain the information and obtain it.
- Determine staff required to obtain information and formulate a solution (team effort provides more input but requires

more time; individual effort allows for speed but provides less knowledge).
- Analyze data and parameters in existence when the problem started.
- Solve the problem.
- Take steps to prevent recurrence.

A complete problem solving scheme can be stated as follows:

A. Identify the problem.
B. How did it occur?
C. Solve it.
D. How will you prevent it from happening again?

Decision Making

You make many decisions every day. Your success and that of your department and your company depend on decision-making ability at all levels. Here are some pointers for making decisions.

Obtain correct information. Rapid decisions are usually desirable, but the decision maker must know whether he has all the facts or needs more information, and he must assess the accuracy of the information he has.

Based on scientific method (1) identify the decision to be made; (2) list the information needed to make a proper decision; (3) list the information you already have; (4) determine what further information is needed; (5) decide how and when to get the further information; and (6) evaluate all the information and make the decision. Keep in mind that some information will be accurate and complete. Some will be accurate and incomplete; get more information. Some information will be erroneous; replace it with correct information. If you encounter an outright lie, replace both the information and the person who lied. Having correct data will enable you to make good decisions.

Training

The importance of training is often overlooked and training is usually the first area to suffer cutbacks when finances are tight. Training is vital and should not be subject to budget cuts or neglect. Training can be conducted internally or by outside providers; the best programs combine both types. Large companies have departments that determine training needs, establish needed programs, and maintain records of employee training and qualifications.

In-house instructors know a company's systems and can apply new information and techniques with ease. External consultants and contractors can provide specialized training, for example, on technical, legal, and regulatory issues. Internal instructors know the company's system of doing things and can apply the new information and techniques to the company system. Unfortunately, some training departments exhibit the Not Invented Here (NIH) Syndrome and believe that they know more about what the employees need than anyone else, and that they can provide all the necessary training. This was discussed in Chapter 17, Current Concepts, Trends, and Tools.

Lack of training is readily apparent in performance. An employee who may appear to lack motivation may simply be untrained. Training should enable staff members to do their jobs properly. If they do not perform well, the reason may be one or more of the following:

1. They don't know why they should do the job.
2. They don't know when to begin and end.
3. They don't know what they are supposed to do.
4. They don't know how to do the job.
5. They think they are doing the job.
6. They think their methods are better or your way won't work.
7. They think something else is more important.
8. They think they can't do the job.
9. They are rewarded for not doing the job.
10. They are not rewarded for doing the job.

In attempting to correct problems related to employee performance, it is important to determine which reason(s) listed above led to the problem. After you find the cause, you can readily handle the solution.

There is another type of training and that is the training offered in the continuing education departments of colleges and universities. This is an interesting type of instruction because, when attending these classes, most students are already in the working world and therefore have work experience to bring to class with them. This is most conducive to everyone learning not only from the instructor but also from the other students.

I asked Dr. Sametria McFall, who directs continuing education at Savannah State University in Georgia, for her comments. She said, "Today's working adults face myriad challenges. In addition to a hectic home life, they are expected to stay on top of and in some instances ahead of the latest technology and information. In this world of rapid information and technology changes, the Department of Continuing Education at Savannah State University helps working adults improve their skills and we keep them up to date on cutting edge professional development. Our classes and workshops are strategically designed to fit today's busy lifestyles without sacrificing quality. In continuing education, we are dedicated to lifelong learning, and this commitment is reflected in everything we do!" Dr. McFall's division serves the needs of working adults (and their employers) in Coastal Georgia and parts of South Carolina.

Priorities

You may know the time management system of assigning A, B, and C priorities to all your tasks, then completing them in alphabetical sequence, starting with A items. C items may not be completed for lack of time, and new A status tasks may require attention. As a result, priorities are shifted and some chores are never completed.

A key point in setting priorities is that your priorities must interface with others' priorities! When priority tasks are not finished, it is not always because the effort has not been expended; it's often because parts of the tasks depended on completion of tasks by others who did not finish on time. No one works in a void; constant interactions are required. Completion of a task requires coordination with other people and their priorities. This is accomplished by talking to them and working toward common goals.

Another key point is that not all important things are urgent; most are not. Importance and urgency require different tactics. Determine whether a task is urgent and important. If it is, schedule it appropriately. If it is important but not urgent, it might be better handled later.

As new tasks appear, you may have to alter your schedule according to their priorities. These suggestions may allow you to accomplish more in a day.

Report Format

Laboratories use report forms to summarize projects. The format shown below can be modified to suit any type of project in any type of business. All reports should be concise but still include necessary details. They provide continuing records of progress, indicate work flow, and point out paths to end results.

Laboratory Report Form

SECTION	INFORMATION
Title	What are you doing?
Objective	Why are you doing it?
Theory	Why do you think it will work?
Reagents and equipment	What do you need?
Procedure	How are you going to do it?
Data	Show data and calculations.
Results	What did you find?
Conclusions	Why did that happen?
Recommendations	What should we do next?

Reference Points

We all use reference points without realizing it. You determine the location of an item by a reference point, for example, a pen on a desk. You are the reference point and determine the distance and direction of the pen. Driving a car requires constant assessment of reference points (your speed, speeds of other drivers, speed limits) and making judgments. Arranging a meeting with another person requires two reference points: time and place. Agreeing to meet at 2 p.m. is worthless unless you know where and on what date. Reference points are also important in your career progression:

- Where am I now?
- Where do I want to go?
- What does it take to get there?

Reference points help you "get there." Observe during your journey, make appropriate changes when needed, and enjoy the ride.

Learn about Yourself

Write a three-page article about any subject. Let it sit for two days and then read it as if you didn't know who wrote it. What does it reveal about the author? Did the author write something interesting, pleasant, angry, sad, general, specific, or analytical? What would you think about the personality of the author if you didn't know him or her?

Learn about Others

You will continually meet many new people in your career and will have to decide which ones will become friends or associates and which ones deserve minimal contact. You cannot make that decision without learning about them. One common technique is to "find out how important people are to me by what they consider is important to them." You learn by listening. Simply say, "Tell me about yourself. What do you like and what do you dislike?" You may be surprised about how readily people will answer and reveal what's most important to them. This allows you to judge how important they will be to you. A person may complain about problems and never mention proposed remedies or mention constructive matters like business or inventions. Let the person talk. You will gain valuable information about how this person will or will not fit into your life.

Teams

Did you ever notice at a business or social function that the groups cluster into classifications, e.g., young, middle-aged, senior? Each group has common characteristics and similar people will gravitate to appropriate groups. For business purposes, such groupings are not productive. At large conventions and company meetings, it is wise to expand your contacts. Mingle with people from whom you can learn. Business events allow you to mix with people from other departments or companies and exchange knowledge.

Diversity goes beyond sex and ethnicity. It also applies to experience and age. When assembling teams and working groups for a particular assignment, managers tend to assign members in a narrow age range, e.g., the 20- to 30-year-old team or the senior team. Younger employees understand the latest technology; more senior employees have an abundance of business experience. Both groups have much knowledge to contribute to a team effort.

Mediocre basketball teams usually have talented players but they all have the same levels of experience and expertise. If they all specialized in three-point shots, the result would be a talented group of players but not necessarily a winning team. A team needs diversity: a distance shooter, a close-up shooter, and a good defensive player who work effectively together.

Apply this principle to a team assembled to bring a new product to the market. You don't need all players with the same talent. You want scientists and engineers who can conceptualize, those who can develop the project and design test procedures, those who can scale a process to pilot plant scale, those who can estimate costs, and those who can market the product. A combination of talent constitutes a well functioning team.

Some managers are misguided in that they stress team performance and then award an individual for his or her accomplishments. This erodes the team concept. If you want to recognize superior effort by a team, acknowledge and reward the entire team.

Dealing with Media

Watch what you say when a microphone is turned on and a camera is rolling. What you say and do during a recording or photography session cannot be retracted. Sports announcers, politicians, actors, law enforcement officials, and others have slipped and said something stupid, controversial, or both that went on the air. Despite prompt apology, the result is a tarnished image. Abraham Lincoln said, it's "better to remain silent and be thought a fool than to speak out and remove all doubt."

Media members know how to goad people into making statements they may regret. Listen carefully to questions, answer briefly and to the point, and never answer trick questions. You don't have to answer every question. By answering a trick question, an inexperienced coach may reveal his game tactics to a reporter and thus to the opposing team.

Question: "Hey coach, what are you specifically going to do to beat the other team this afternoon? What's your game plan?"

Correct answer: "Come on now, you know better than to ask me that just before the game. What other questions do you have?"

The inexperienced coach may reveal his game tactics to the reporter and the audience and now the opposing team knows them and can formulate how to counter those tactics.

It's really easy to make a good presentation. Don't ruin it by saying too much about things you weren't going to talk about. Know in advance what you will and what you will not talk about.

Measurements

Modern business tends to measure the easiest parameters rather than the most relevant. Measurements may be accurate but not meaningful and you should understand what they mean and how valuable they are. Sports announcers and political analysts excel in disseminating meaningless statistics. They toss numbers at you that have no significance but fill plenty of air time.

A football announcer may say that a quarterback has thrown passes up to 10 yards 27% of the time, 10 to 20 yards 52% of the time, and more than 20 yards 21% of the time this season. That information doesn't matter because the opponent's defense for this game is different from previous teams' defenses, and the quarterback may change his pattern. Readers trained to read business and technical material know that several parameters must be defined before a valid pattern is visible and predictions can be made.

Measurements may be called *metrics*—a widely used but unclear "buzz" term that can be used to mask incomplete or irrelevant measurements. Knowing what metrics to have and knowing what to do with them is another story. Be sure you have the proper metrics.

Example 1—A restaurant measures the number of customers and the times of day they arrived. This measurement does not indicate how many customers left before being seated because no host or hostess acknowledged them.

Example 2—Plant manager performance is measured by the number and value of units shipped from each facility (see Chapter 17). Are returned goods subtracted from units shipped?

Example 3—A marketing firm advertises through pop-up ads on the Internet listing the number of ads and the number of persons reached. Does the firm consider the people who, because of the distraction caused by the ads, resolve to not buy their product or service and will also advise friends not to buy them?

When you review measurements and statistics, look beyond what is measured most readily. Determine what parameters are significant and measure them even if it requires more effort.

Miscellany

Communicating

What do you want to say?
To whom do you want to say it?
Do you have their attention?

Selling

What is your product (define specifically)?
Why should someone buy your product?
Why should they buy from you and not from your competitors?

Three Rs

Respect for yourself
Respect for others
Responsibility for your actions

The Three Worlds

The world the way it should be.
The world the way you want it to be.
The world the way it is. (This is the one you live in.)

People

Little people talk about people.
Average people talk about things.
Superior people talk about ideas.

Unsolved Problems

Problems that go away by themselves often come back by themselves.

Counterproductive Behavior

One of the symptoms of insanity is to do the same thing over and over the same way and expect a different result.

Goals

Goals are dreams with deadlines.

Final Thoughts

Always keep your word. If through unforeseen circumstance you believe that you cannot keep your word, tell your client, supervisor, employee, etc. the reason. In Shakespeare's *Hamlet*, Polonius tells his son, Laertes, "This above all: to thine own self be true. And it must follow, as the night the day, thou canst not then be false to any man."

You can learn about science and business and projects and relationships, but your principles should follow the Golden Rule: *Do unto others as you would have them do unto you.*

Index

For Product Safety Concerns and Information please contact our EU
representative GPSR@taylorandfrancis.com Taylor & Francis Verlag GmbH,
Kaufingerstraße 24, 80331 München, Germany

Printed and bound by CPI Group (UK) Ltd, Croydon, CR0 4YY
08/05/2025
01864425-0002